THE SECRET TO AWESOMENESS

Creating the Life You've Always Wanted

Joshua Tongol

Also by Joshua Tongol

SO YOU THOUGHT YOU KNEW

Letting Go of Religion

First Printing, 2015

ISBN 978-0-9914639-5-4 (Paperback)
ISBN 978-0-9914639-4-7 (Kindle)

Book Design by Brother Teresa
cargocollective.com/brotherteresa

Joshua Tongol
joshuatongol.com

To those who dare to believe...

CONTENTS

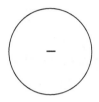

A PAINFUL DISGUISE...

"Stop acting so small.
You are the universe in ecstatic motion."
Rumi

"You will never do anything in this world without courage.
It is the greatest quality of the mind next to honor."
Aristotle

It was 2006.

There I was in the university auditorium, nervously standing in front of a crowd of college students. All of them were waiting for me to say something. Anything. Little did they know, I was facing one of my life's greatest and oldest fears. And no, I'm not talking about public speaking. It was something else.

Why the hell am I doing this? I was thinking. *Why now? I mean, I've gotten so used to not doing it for so long, is there really any point in giving it another try?*

The thing is, something happened to me right before I was called up front to speak that totally screwed up my original plan for the evening.

All I wanted to do was tell the audience about a *radical paradigm shift* I had experienced several months prior. It was a shift that messed me up so bad (in a good way) that it changed the way I saw …
life,
the world,
and even myself.

To sum it all up, it was basically this idea:

All things—including miracles—are possible
to those who believe.

Although I was excited to share this life-changing truth with everyone, remember, this unexpected "thing" happened to me at what I thought was the "worst" possible time.

You see, even though I had started to believe that anything is possible, there was one thing in particular that *felt* impossible. I had a "limitation," so to speak. One *I* had created for myself. *Talk about cognitive dissonance!*

And now, without much preparation, and in front of all these people, I was actually gonna try to overcome this "limitation" I had. There was so much weighing on this. I just knew deep down, if I actually succeeded, it wouldn't just be a breakthrough for other people, but it would also be a breakthrough that I desperately needed for myself.

Then ... without warning ... I found myself bursting into tears.

There I stood ... vulnerable ... with every eye in the room fixed upon me ... feeling like I was helpless. I tried overcoming my fear several times, but I just couldn't. And soon enough, as my mind began to be overwhelmed with painful childhood memories, the fear deepened even more—rising along with what seemed like the inevitable conclusion of being a failure. Right there. In front of all those people.

Suddenly, at what seemed to come out of nowhere, a courage from deep within made an unexpected appearance.

And then ...

it happened.

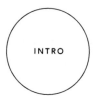

INTRO

WHAT DO YOU SEE?

"When you change the way you look at things,
the things you look at change."
Wayne Dyer

"If the doors of perception were cleansed,
everything would appear to man as it is, Infinite."
William Blake

The great physicist Albert Einstein once said that one of the most important decisions we could ever make is whether we believe we live in a friendly or hostile universe.

Why? Because our beliefs matter.

Whether we realize it or not, they function as a pair of glasses, so to speak—mental lenses—enabling us to see the world in a certain way. And based on how we see the universe as being either friendly or hostile, will definitely affect the way we live our lives.

Think of it another way.

When you wake up everyday, what do you mostly see in your world?

Do you see *love?*
Or do you see *fear?*

'Cause these two, believe it or not,
are the primary lenses through which we see the world.

But before I start asking you too many questions, let me tell you a little bit about what I saw in *my world* for many years.

o o o

For most of my life, the ability to see everything through the lens of love was more of a challenge than a possibility.

Like everyone else, I've had my own share of crap to deal with. And with this crap came fear, which blinded me from seeing the good in so many situations. (If you get what I'm saying, go ahead and breathe a big sigh of relief. It officially confirms you're not alone.)

To throw it out there already, I was born with an underdeveloped right hand. A deformity. This led me to become extremely self-conscious about it. I felt ugly, embarrassed and definitely inadequate on the inside. Unfortunately, this sucky feeling of being "different" affected me for years on end.

The way I saw myself physically wasn't all I had to deal with as a kid though. In addition to my insecurities, I also grew up as a religious fundamentalist. As is common among many of them, I suffered a lot from guilt and shame—thinking that a "loving" (and angry) God in the sky was always disappointed in me whenever I screwed up. Sadly, this understanding made me afraid of "him" from time to time.

○ ○ ○

During my teenage years, I went from one odd job to another—from telemarketing (selling newspapers) to doing security at events. The sad thing is that I wasn't exactly enjoying what I was doing. Once I reached college, I felt like I had no sense of purpose, no direction, and no passion. In other words, I had no freakin' clue what I wanted to do with my life.

Luckily, as time went on, I eventually found a good (yet

challenging) job, achieved financial stability, and even attended a reputable private school. There were also plenty of other things to be thankful for: family, friends, food, clothes, a new car, and even a decent apartment.

What could've possibly gone wrong?

Well, in 2005, I was diagnosed with a chronic digestive disease. But that wasn't all. I also suffered from excruciating pain related to a back injury. From then on, one negative thing led to another, and my life kept spiraling down from there.

The pain I experienced day in and day out—both physically and emotionally—was sometimes unbearable. I'd constantly ask God the "Why me?" question, thinking life was unfair.

I didn't know what to believe anymore. Life had hit an all-time low. I felt confused … hopeless … but most of all … afraid. I feared that, as a young man, my body (and life) would never be the same again.

What I discovered back in 2006 was absolutely *the* turning point for me. It was the beginning of something special. It was a journey of …
ideas,
faith,
and victories.

Since then, my life has never been the same …
for the better that is.

As I write this, it's now the year 2014. I'm married to a very beautiful and supportive woman. I'm feeling healthier and stronger than ever. I travel the world, making a positive impact on people's lives. But most of all, I'm learning to actually love myself, and getting what every word of that actually means for a change. And from this self-love, thankfully, my whole outlook on life has been transformed (and is still changing).

Now, don't get me wrong, life is still a process for me (as it is for all of us). I'm not gonna pretend I've got it all figured out or act like I'm the complete package. *Ha! That would be the day!* But then again, I'm not stupid enough to say I didn't grow or learn a couple things along the path that brought me to where I'm at now.

o o o

In this book, I'm gonna be challenging long-held ideas that I believe might be *hurting* rather than *helping* you. I'll be offering you alternative ideas—another pair of glasses, as it were— through which you can see the world. And this other way of "seeing" will not only benefit you, but the rest of humanity as well.

You see, every generation has its own built-in assumptions—even ours. For example, we've been told by family, friends, and educators …
what to believe and what *not* to believe,
what's possible and what's *impossible,*
what's scientific and what's science *fiction.*

And because our assumptions are the basis for all we experience, whichever assumptions we end up believing will inevitably determine everything we "see." And everything we see, believe it or not, will end up creating our reality.

Thing is, many of us haven't even thought about questioning the assumptions handed down to us—even when we started noticing their limiting (and sometimes negative) effects on our lives. (Don't worry, I'll discuss more of this later.)

We let the experts answer our questions,
but never thought about questioning any of their answers.

The results?

We've settled for what's considered to be "normal."
We've settled for life functioning in a certain way.
We've settled for being "realistic."

We've settled, period.

Why?

If our perceptions *determine* and *create* our lives, then why should we settle for anything less than what we desire? What I mean is, if we're unhappy with the results our beliefs have led us to, then why not finally be open to different beliefs other than the second-hand ones we've settled for too easily?

So once again, at this time in your life, what do you see?

And are there things in your life you'd want to change?

You did pick up this book for a reason, right?

Maybe you're ...
constantly getting sick ...
barely making ends meet ...
always worried, longing for peace ...
filthy rich, but feeling empty inside ...
"successful," but hate who you've become.

Whatever your situation is, ask yourself: *Am I gonna accept everything "as is"? Have I reached a point where "enough is enough"? Am I willing to do whatever it takes to bring about the desired changes in my life?*

Think about it. If you keep doing the same things you've always done up to this point, should you be surprised if you keep getting the same results? Did you know the definition of "insanity" is doing the same thing over and over again and expecting different results? If that's the case, shouldn't you start thinking and doing things differently in order to bring about the results you *really* want?

○ ○ ○

As you read along, what I'm asking you to do is to think "outside the box," so to speak—to be open to a radically new way of thinking *and* living. When I say "radical," it's not necessarily because it is (in my opinion). It's radical because it might be different from what is commonly understood by many "realistic" people today.

The truths you're about to discover in this book can work for absolutely anyone. *(Yes, even you!)* It doesn't matter who you are, what you've done, or even what religion (or worldview) you identify with.

Why?

The Universe plays no favorites.

Does this surprise you? Sound too good to be true? Still wrestling with doubt? Are you like, "Nah, this stuff won't work for me." If so, then keep reading, 'cause we'll be working on that attitude in just a moment.

I know we're all at different places along our journey in life. I get that. And some of us are more open to certain ideas than others which is totally fine. That being said, I think this book will bring out three different types of reactions:

1. *"No way! This is New Age woo-woo!"*
2. *"We must expose these lies!"*
3. *"This makes so much sense!"*

Whatever *your* internal reactions might be, consider what some philosopher-dude named Arthur Schopenhauer said when it comes to truth. He states that all truth basically goes through three steps.

First, it is *ridiculed.*
Second, it is violently *opposed.*
Finally, it is accepted as *self-evident.*

Keep in mind that for several years I myself ridiculed and opposed the very ideas contained in this book. I wasn't just on the other side of the fence, I practically lived there for so long, I didn't even think I could ever move away! So I definitely know what it's like to be a skeptic *and* a critic of what I'm about to share.

As for my reasons, to be honest, it was initially difficult for me to accept these radical ideas at first. They contradicted a lot of what I was taught and even more so, what I believed for many years. They just seemed too "out there," too "impossible" for me to swallow. To confirm my doubt even more, neither did I have any experiences to back up if these ideas really "worked" anyway.

Anyone who believed such "New Agey" ideas were, in my mind, "gullible" or "unintelligent." With a genuine care for others, I did my best to expose these "lies" and save people from their delusions. In other words, if you knew me back then, I wasn't the one who *passively* disagreed with these ideas, I *passionately* disagreed with them!

Thankfully, and it was definitely a process, things began to change once I became more open to other ideas *other* than my own. You see, as a student of life, I wanna know the truth—even if it means letting go of some long-held beliefs.

So I eventually put these ideas (principles) to the test in my own life because I didn't want it to be all theory to me. I wanted to experience its *true* reality.

My conclusion: (Pardon my French)
This … s#!% … works.

The truth is, these ideas aren't even new (just new to some folks). So I'm not claiming originality here. I'll admit, I'm standing on the shoulders of giants who came way before me—men and women—who didn't just teach these ideas, they lived them out in their lives—inspiring countless people around the world.

These are peeps such as …
Wallace Wattles,
Napoleon Hill,
Joseph Murphy,
Florence Shinn,
Norman Peale,
Neville Goddard,
Earl Nightingale,
and more.

These thought leaders were ahead of their time. They challenged the status quo by stepping out of its ranks. They had the guts to demonstrate what they believed to be true—despite their critics.

As I read their various works, I thought, *"Dude! Why don't more people know about this?"*—which helped birth this book you now hold in your hands.

I'll also be bringing together ideas from various quantum physicists, futurists, motivational speakers, contemporary thought leaders, and spiritual teachers. And of course I'll be adding my own flavor and experiences too.

○ ○ ○

I know it's not something you usually hear everyday, but I'm here to *remind* you of how awesome and amazingly powerful you really are.

There's a Power within you, an Intelligence—an Invisible Consciousness—capable of infinite possibilities. All I'm doing here is showing you how to "connect" to this Source. And with this knowledge, along with some practical tips, you'll be empowered to create the life you've always wanted.

But the first step is to take 100% responsibility for your life right now. Get rid of any "victim mentality." If you're not going to be the boss of your own life, then that position will be filled without your permission.

You don't need to wait for a serious crisis to happen.

You don't need to wait till rock bottom smacks you hard in the face.

Now is the time …
to discover what really makes you happy.

Now is the time …
to find the courage to do things you never thought possible.

Now is the time …
to follow your dreams no matter what the critics say.

Now is the time …
to tap into what the human spirit is supposed to do.

Now is the time …
to "grow a greater you."[1]

Sure, some skeptics might say this is all a bunch of B.S. But you know what?—let 'em talk. I love the Chinese proverb that says,

> "The person who says it cannot be done
> should not interrupt the person doing it."

Let the skeptics be skeptics. People usually criticize what they don't understand or haven't experienced anyway (like me in the past). It's easier for them to talk smack than to actually take the risk themselves. But then again, this isn't about them. (If it is, that's where half the misery comes from.)

This is about *you*.

So find out the truth for yourself.
Be open to "new" beliefs.

And see just how far you're willing to go.

We're all *writing* and *creating* the stories that make up our lives. And if you don't like the chapter you're currently in, then guess what?

It's time to rewrite it.

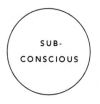

SUB-
CONSCIOUS

"I HAVE TWO WHAT?!"

"I will not let anyone walk through my mind
with their dirty feet."
Mahatma Gandhi

"You are today where your thoughts have brought you;
you will be tomorrow where your thoughts take you."
James Allen

You know how the story goes.

It's the end of the year. You're excited. Motivated like crazy. Nothing can stop you now. You're finally gonna do it. So you grab a pen and paper.

At the top of the page, you write *"New Year's Resolution."*

You start jotting things down. The list begins.

1. Lose 50 lbs.
2. Quit smoking
3. Control my anger

Then … the new year begins.

A few days go by and you haven't lit up a cigarette. (*I got this!*)

Two weeks race past and you've lost three pounds. (*Woohoo!*)

An entire month goes by and you haven't yelled at anyone. (*Piece of cake!*)

Then … two months pass.

A cigarette's in one hand.
A fork's in the other (using it to eat an *entire* cake).
And you're pissed off at yourself for not sticking to the plan.

Fail.

OK, so maybe the New Year doesn't look like this for everyone. But I think you get my drift. We all want to improve our lives for the better in any way, shape or form—whether it's through the use of positive thinking, writing down goals, saying magical prayers, or even will-power.

But why don't our methods always work?
And why do we sometimes get the exact opposite of what we desire?

Here's why:

We have *two* minds.
(No, I didn't say "two brains" so no need to freak out.)

First off, we have something called the *conscious* mind. And second, we also have something called the *subconscious* mind.

Now, if the idea of having "two minds" still freaks you out, then think of it instead as having *two spheres of activity within one mind*. Is that better? OK, let's move on.

Wait, before I get into that, let's go back in time—to the beginning— let's say, to when you first came into this world as a baby. You were this innocent bundle of joy, weren't you? You were constantly living only in the present—not distracted by the problems of the world at all. You weren't concerned with ethics, politics or even religion. It was a time when life was pretty much, well, worry-free.

As a child—between your toddler and preschool years—the world was one big playground to you. If you were buck-naked, it didn't matter—you'd still run around the house without shame. If you picked your nose and found something slimy or crusty—whatever you discovered was food. If you saw a puddle of mud, you'd jump in and play—not giving a rip of what others would say. You did things ... well ... just because.

And then you got older.

As you started becoming more aware of your surroundings, people started telling you what was right and wrong—good and bad—acceptable and unacceptable—possible and impossible.

"Thin is better."
"Dancing is a sin."
"Miracles don't exist."
"God hates homosexuals."
"Left-handedness is abnormal."
"You can't do what you love and make a living."

Then ... in that teeny-tiny brain of yours ... without you even realizing it ... guess what was happening?—countless downloads of beliefs.

Well, it's not just you. All of us have inherited other people's beliefs without our permission—no exceptions. The source of our beliefs could've come from our parents, teachers, movie stars, musicians, television—basically anybody with any kind of influence in our lives. Whether or not our sources had good intentions, well, that doesn't even matter. We still got affected one way or another.

According to contemporary thought leader Gregg Braden, in his book *The Spontaneous Healing of Belief*, he mentions the fact that up until the age of seven, the human brain is in some sort of dreamlike state—meaning, the mind is very impressionable. It basically absorbs everything around it—like a sponge—soaking in one idea after another. (Which is why we gotta be extra careful with what we say and do, especially around children!)

It makes sense when you think about it. Should any of us be surprised if we get caught acting or thinking like our parents? I mean, throughout the "sponge years," I'm sure we've picked up a couple of things here and there—habits of theirs—both good and bad. We probably don't see them at times, but truth is, our friends most likely noticed them first.

o o o

OK, now back to the whole conscious and subconscious distinction.

The conscious (or objective) mind is the *rational* mind. It's the voluntary mind which analyzes all the information and actually *decides*. In other words, it's the mind which chooses what school you're gonna attend, whom you're gonna marry, and what you're gonna eat for dinner tomorrow.

The subconscious (or subjective) mind, on the other hand, is the *irrational* mind. It doesn't think and choose the same way the conscious mind does. Instead, it reacts based on the information stored in it. But don't let that trick you into thinking it's the weaker one of the two. Nothing could be further from the truth.

In fact, William James, the father of American psychology, said the power to move the world is in your subconscious mind. It's your subconscious impressions which *determine* your world. Now, if what he said is true, well then, understanding how your subconscious mind works seems to be pretty darn important, I must say.

You see, your subconscious mind works 24/7. It never sleeps. It's so important that it orchestrates all of your bodily functions without you consciously choosing—from pumping blood, to digesting food, and even breathing. Imagine waking up every morning and having to say, "Hello there, heart, do you mind beating rhythmically today?" Or imagine having to remind yourself when to breathe. Dude, if these things only functioned when you consciously put some effort into them, then it's safe to say you'd probably be dead now!

There's another interesting thing about your subconscious mind as well. According to the late metaphysical author, Robert Collier, he said, "Our subconscious minds have no sense of humor, play no jokes, and cannot tell the difference between reality and an imagined thought or image." That is to say, your subconscious mind has no filter—it's completely impersonal. It doesn't hear a negative belief and argue with it. It doesn't even care whether or not a belief is true.

What your subconscious mind does accept as true—
and this is very important to remember—
is whatever you *feel* to be true.

Let me give you an example of how powerful the "truth" in your subconscious mind is. You wake up early in the morning and read your daily [positive] affirmation book. (To some it's called a "devotional.") Once you finish reading this uplifting book, you shut it—feel inspired—and believe today is gonna be a good day.

But thirty minutes later, what seems to come "out of nowhere," you feel like crap. You're like, "What happened? Why do I suddenly feel this way for no reason?"

Well, there actually is a reason. It's simple. Your good ol' subconscious mind started kicking in. See, although you did some "positive mind preparation" in the morning, which is good, here's another important thing to remember:

You operate from your subconscious mind 95% of the time!

Let me explain it further. Take driving for instance. Growing up in the Middle East, my wife never learned how to drive a car. I still remember the first time she started learning to drive here in America—her conscious mind was aware of almost everything around her—her speed, the traffic lights, street signs, etc. Being in the passenger seat, I'd hardly say anything to her because I didn't wanna be a distraction. Another way of putting it is ... well ... I didn't wanna be in a car crash!

With much repetition and practice, her driving skills improved. Nowadays, she can easily get from point A to point B, engage in a conversation, and not have to be fully aware of everything around her as she drives.

So the question is, *Who does the driving if she's not fully aware of her surroundings?* You guessed it—the good ol' subconscious mind again! It naturally takes over. I'm not saying she can drive with her eyes closed. (Please don't try it unless you want interesting results.) But I think you get what I'm saying.[1]

o o o

Your subconscious mind has a record of everything, I mean *everything*—every thought, every emotion, every encouragement—all the highs—all the lows—pretty much everything we've ever experienced in our lifetime.

Even though most of you don't even remember a particular argument you had, let's say, ten years ago, every part of that experience is still there in your subconscious mind. Call it your own mental USB drive, if you will, except you don't have to consciously choose to save anything. Your subconscious mind *automatically* saves everything for you.

This is why "positive thinking" only gets you so far. It's good and all, don't get me wrong. But what's more important are the beliefs *behind* the positive thoughts—the ones rooted in your subconscious mind. 'Cause they're the ones that really run the show. Trust me, no matter how many positive thoughts you try and muster up, it doesn't matter, the negative beliefs in your subconscious mind always win.

Which is why Mommy and Daddy, in their moment of anger, should've thought twice before calling you "stupid," or telling you they wish you were never born, or saying you'd never amount to anything. Sure, they might've said those hurtful words to you decades ago, but remember, those painful memories are still there in your subconscious mind and can be triggered at any time.

o o o

The power of suggestion also plays a role in all this. For example, what if someone looks at you and says, "Hey, you don't look too good. Are you feeling sick? I think you should go see a doctor." Guess what? Depending on how susceptible you are to suggestion, even if you weren't sick to begin with, you can actually begin to *feel* sick. And it's not because you actually are sick, it's because you *accept the suggestion* that you are sick. Seriously, that's how powerful a suggestion can be once your subconscious mind accepts it to be true—even if it's not.

I remember an eye-opening demonstration on the power of

suggestion given by hypnotist/mentalist Derren Brown. In one of his videos, he brought a woman to a forest to show her the "power" of a voodoo doll.

Derren told the woman, "The thing about this doll is that it doesn't have a soul. So we need to give it a soul for this to work." She *agreed*. Derren then grabbed the woman's hand, appeared to take the ring off her finger, then put the ring in a little compartment inside the center of the voodoo doll to become its soul.

Derren turned around—with his back facing toward the woman—and began to wrap yarn tightly around the bottom half of the doll. Then he asked her if she felt anything. The woman was terribly shocked to discover she couldn't move her legs.

Derren turned around again to face her and said, "You can move your arms, yes?"—and she began flapping her arms up and down with ease. But while her arms were flapping, Derren began wrapping the yarn tightly around the top half of the doll—and slowly, but surely, she was suddenly unable to move her arms.

Then, Derren asked her to count from ten to zero out loud. As she began counting backward, he wrapped the yarn tightly around the neck of the doll. This time, as I'm sure you've figured it out by now, she was suddenly unable to speak.

Next, Derren said, "The only reason why you can't speak

is that you believe you can't speak … because of what I'm telling you. The interesting thing is that if I tell you you [sic] can speak, all that does is give you permission to question that belief and then you find that you can speak."

At that instant the woman suddenly spoke.

Even more to her surprise, Derren explained to her that it's not even a real voodoo doll, but that the trick was to get her to *invest in the belief* that it was a real voodoo doll—by investing something of herself in it, namely, her ring.

Derren unwrapped the center of the voodoo doll, and to her surprise again, she noticed the ring wasn't even there.

So what happened to the ring? Did it magically disappear?

Nope. As Derren later revealed in the video, he never put the ring inside the voodoo doll in the first place. In other words, the ring was on her finger the entire time!

You see, there was no power in the voodoo doll whatsoever. Rather, the power came from the woman's *agreement* (belief) with Derren's suggestions.

o o o

There's another story I love sharing which is found in Joseph Murphy's classic book *The Power of Your Subconscious Mind.* A friend of his, Dr. Evelyn Fleet, told him about an article which appeared in English newspapers. It shows how obedient the subconscious mind can be even when it comes to certain figures of speech we use.

Here's what happened in Joseph's own words:

> *This is the suggestion a man gave to his subconscious mind over a period of about two years: "I would give my right arm to see my daughter cured." It appeared that his daughter had a crippling form of arthritis together with the so called* [sic] *incurable form of skin disease. Medical treatment had failed to alleviate the condition, and the father had an intense longing for his daughter's healing, and expressed his desire in the words just quoted.*

As the rest of the story goes, one day the family was out driving. (Can you see where this is going?) They crashed into another car and the father's right arm was immediately torn off at the shoulder. But check this out … at the same time the father's arm was torn off … get this … are you ready?—*the daughter's arthritis and skin condition vanished!*

Now that's not a happy story, well, for the father, that is. But it comes to show just how powerful suggestion really is. Or to be more specific, if you say something enough times, coupled with emotions, it allows for the suggestion to sink into your subconscious mind … then *BAM!*—it becomes your reality.

o o o

OK, on a more positive note, Emile Coue, author of *Self Mastery Through Autosuggestion*, understood the power of suggestion as well—using it to help others help themselves. His well-known mantra, "Everyday, in every way, I'm getting better and better," has helped cure thousands of people from illnesses.

That said, I strongly suggest you say positive affirmations all throughout the day—everyday. I also suggest saying them right before going to bed or first thing when waking up (or both!). Why? 'Cause when you're in a much drowsier and passive state of mind, your mind is less argumentative and much more receptive to suggestion.

Then once the positive affirmations seep into your subconscious mind, you'll have new beliefs. And once you have new beliefs, you'll have new feelings, new manifestations, new experiences, new habits—in other words, a completely new way of living!

o o o

Later in this book, I'll be dealing with several major areas of life where many of us struggle with false and self-limiting beliefs. As you read, you might hear ideas which are at odds with some of your current beliefs. It's OK. Keep your heart open, and keep reading. Allow your mind to be stretched to the point of it being renewed. You'll start noticing your faith getting stronger, and you'll be empowered to overcome any "impossible-looking" situation.

At this time, take a moment to think of all the areas of your life (e.g., health, finances, family) you want to see differently. (Seriously, take a couple of minutes to think about it.)

Then ask yourself these questions:

- Why do you think these areas are the way they are?
- What might be the self-limiting beliefs that contribute to these areas?

Now, I'm not asking you to beat yourself up with a guilt trip. I'm just asking you to be aware of these areas you need to work on so you can get started on doing something about them. 'Cause if you're at least aware of any problem, trust me, you're already a step ahead of a lot of people.

So get ready … life's gonna get a helluva lot better from here on out.

Now turn (or swipe) the page, and let me continue showing you how to create your reality.

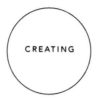

CREATING

BENDING REALITY 101

"Reality is merely an illusion,
albeit a very persistent one."
Mahatma Gandhi

"If you want to find the secrets of the universe,
think in terms of energy, frequency and vibration."
Nikola Tesla

There's a classic scene in the film *The Matrix* (1999) where the main character, Neo (Keanu Reeves), meets someone named Morpheus (Laurence Fishburne) for the first time.[1]

Morpheus: I imagine that right now you're feeling a bit like Alice. Tumbling down the rabbit hole?

Neo: You could say that.

Morpheus: … Do you believe in fate, Neo?

Neo: No.

Morpheus: Why not?

Neo: 'Cause I don't like the idea that I'm not in control of my life.

Morpheus: … You're here because you know something. … Do you know what I'm talking about?

Neo: The Matrix?

Morpheus: Do you want to know what it is?

(Neo nods his head)

Morpheus: The Matrix is everywhere, it is all around us. … It is the world that has been pulled over your eyes to blind you from the truth.

Neo: What truth?

Morpheus: ... You have to see it for yourself. This is your last chance. After this, there is no turning back.

(Morpheus shows a blue pill in his left hand)

You take the blue pill ... the story ends ... you wake in your bed and believe whatever you want to believe.

(He shows a red pill in his right hand.)

You take the red pill ... you stay in Wonderland and I show you how deep the rabbit hole goes. Remember—all I'm offering is the truth, nothing more.

(Neo takes the red pill and swallows it with a glass of water.)

Morpheus: Follow me.

In the film, the choice between the two pills gave Neo the opportunity to either remain ignorant of the truth about reality, or to wake up to it.

So now my first question to you is, *What is reality?*

And my second question is, *Are you ready to hear the truth?*

'Cause whatever reality is, let me tell ya, it isn't what it seems.

Come … follow me down the rabbit hole.

○ ○ ○

Before I begin, I want you to stomp your foot on the ground.

It's solid, right?

Next, I want you to squeeze this book in your hands.

It's solid too, right?

Wrong.

In fact, *you* aren't solid either. (Break out the *Twilight Zone* theme song, please.) I know, I know, it sounds like I'm being silly here. But I'm not.

Let me explain.

You see, according to quantum physics (which deals with the very small stuff), everything we once thought was physical is, well, not physical.

Everything is energy—
the chair you're sitting on,
the house you live in,
the person next to you,
and even your dog.

Sounds crazy, right?

You might be thinking, *"Wait a minute, Josh. But this book in my hands feels physical. How can you say that everything is energy? Quit messing with me before I give you a solid right hook to your physical face!"*

Now, before you try knocking me out to prove me wrong, let me respond with a quote from the book *What the Bleep Do We Know!?* where one author states this mind-bending truth:

> One of the first cracks in the structure of Newtonian physics was the discovery that atoms, the supposedly solid building blocks of the physical universe, were mostly made up of empty space. ... Well, not really. That supposed "emptiness" is not empty at all: It contains enormous quantities of subtle, powerful energy.

Did you get that? Even the so-called "empty space" between atoms isn't really empty either. That, too, is energy.

What I'm basically trying to say is this:
"physical" reality ...
is simply ...
an ...
illusion.

I know this can be hard a pill to swallow. But in case you're wondering why you're having "physical experiences," it's because atoms (which are composed of electrons) repel each other. That is to say, the electrical repulsion of electrons give you the sensation of feeling something. This is why your book isn't slipping through your fingers right now, or why it's probably not a good idea to jump in front of a moving bus.[1]

○ ○ ○

Another crucial feature of quantum physics is the fact that energy can act as either *visible* particles or *invisible* waves.

But get this—and this is where it gets even weirder—it all depends on what you're *looking* for.

What do I mean?

If you're looking for a particle, it becomes a particle.
If you're looking for a wave, it becomes a wave.

Or, as Penney Peirce, author of *Frequency*, puts it:

> "Your perception determines the shape of your reality."

You see, there's something *subjective* about the nature of reality where we have an inescapable influence in constructing it. In fact, contrary to what many people believe, the material world doesn't preexist in any certain form waiting to be observed. Rather, it's the very act of observing which creates the material world. Before then, what exists are fields of possibilities (oceans of waves/frequencies).

For instance, when an observation is made, matter appears—*creating* the world we *perceive*. But when we look away … *BAM!*—it disappears back into energy.

Lynne McTaggert, author of *The Field*, puts it this way:

> Reality is unset Jell-O. There's a big indeterminate sludge out there that's our potential life. And we, by our very active involvement, our act of noticing, our observation, we get that Jell-O to set. So we're intrinsic to the whole process of reality. Our involvement creates that reality.[2]

I guess you could say this ends up blurring the distinction between the world "out there" and the "objective observer."

How crazy is that!

Still not convinced yet? Well, what about when the eminent American theoretical physicist John Wheeler (a colleague of Albert Einstein) said, "We are not simply bystanders on a cosmic stage; we are shapers and creators living in a participatory universe."

"Shapers."
"Creators."

I like that. It's empowering, isn't it?

We all play a decisive part in this …

open,
dynamic …
and interactive …
universe which is constantly changing.

Yup, we are *that* involved!
You can *observe* the life you want!

But the critic can say, "OK, so we can influence the 'small stuff' like subatomic particles. Big deal. But we can't influence the 'big stuff'—like the things we experience in our everyday world."

My response is, *Why not?*

Maybe many of us don't influence the "big stuff" because, as Dr. Joe Dispenza says in his book *Evolve Your Brain*, we're simply "poor observers." But hey, maybe with some practice, we'll be able to influence our reality in more ways than some people expect.

Shouldn't this excite us?

Now high-five the person next to you!

o o o

It's been said that we think around 60,000 thoughts each day. (Don't make me ask what most of yours are about!—wink, wink.) And every thought we have emits a certain frequency.

Positive thoughts vibrate at a higher frequency,
while negative thoughts vibrate at a lower frequency?

Why is this so important?

Well, whatever thought vibrations you're putting "out there" (positive or negative), things of the same frequency will match it back. In other words, your reality—in many ways—is a reflection of your dominant thoughts, which is why being optimistic is so important.

o o o

Earl Nightingale, author of the classic book *The Strangest Secret*, knew that our thoughts had the power to shape our lives—even to the point where they can either "make us or break us."

Earl's famous words were:
"We become what we think about."

Or what about when American poet, Ralph Waldo Emerson, said "A man is what he thinks about all day long." Or when Thomas Merton, the Christian mystic, said he prays by breathing.

You see, what Nightingale, Emerson and Merton believed about our thoughts confirms what many wise teachers, prophets and philosophers have said throughout the ages.

Thoughts and beliefs are life.

Obviously, we have more thoughts than we can actually keep track of, but remember, it's our dominant thoughts which tend to color and create everything we see—which is why we gotta make the thoughts we want the most dominant ones.

○ ○ ○

In addition to thoughts, our *words* are extremely powerful as well. In fact, words do matter … literally. They shape our lives for the good and for the bad—depending, of course, on how we use them.

As a kid, I remember being on the playground and hearing my classmates say, "Sticks and stones will break my bones. But words will never hurt me."

Well … that's not necessarily true.

Consider the well-known water experiment done by Japanese researcher, Dr. Masaru Emoto. In his popular book, *The Hidden Messages in Water*, he reveals how words have the power to influence water.

In the experiment, he exposed water to different types of music, prayers and words. Using high-speed photography, he visually captured the structure of water at the moment of freezing.

The results were freakin' eye-opening!

For example, when he exposed water to positive words such as "love," "thank you," and the like, the water formed beautiful crystals (like snowflakes). But when he exposed water to negative words such as "I hate you," "you idiot," "you make me sick," "I will kill you,"—the water, interestingly so, formed dark holes, dull colors—and became, in a word, ugly.

How does this have anything to do with us?

Think about it. What percentage of the human body is composed of water? Oh, that's right, it's over 70%! That being said, wouldn't it be a good idea to be very careful with what we say *to* and *about* ourselves?

o o o

Like thoughts and words, our *feelings* play a vital role in creating our reality too. Not only do they reveal what we're vibrating at any moment, but they also indicate what we believe as "truth" in our subconscious minds—even if our beliefs are *not* true.

For instance, some of us have written down positive affirmations on sticky-notes like "I'm rich!" or "I'm healthy," posting them all over our bathroom mirrors, our computer screens, and around our office cubicle at work—reciting them over and over again—hoping to see our affirmations become a reality.

The results?

They hardly did us any good.

Sometimes, they helped. And other times, unfortunately, they didn't.

Why?

'Cause we weren't "feeling the words."[3]

Our lips said one thing,
but our feelings expressed the exact opposite.

You could shout all the positive declarations you want till the cows come home for all I care. But if you don't say them enough to the point of affecting your subconscious mind, and without any emotions behind them, then don't expect too much to happen.

Remember: *words, coupled with emotion, are power.*[4]

o o o

This leads me to my next point,
a proper understanding of *faith*.

Unfortunately, many skeptics tend to scorn faith—thinking it's for those who are irrational, weak-minded and gullible. (I guess it all depends on how one defines it, right?)

As for me, real faith proves just the opposite. It's for those who are able to rationalize beyond the limiting beliefs many people tend to embrace. In fact, it can take a lot of cojones to have the kind of faith I'm talking about in certain situations.

See, not only do I have several anecdotal stories to back up my understanding of faith, but the kind of faith I'm suggesting is also supported by the idea that *all possibilities exist in the present moment.*

Let me share a powerful example of this.

I'll never forget the story in Gregg Braden's book *The Isaiah Effect* where he talks about his trip to the desert of northern New Mexico with his Native American friend David.[5]

As the story goes, it was the third year of drought in the American Desert Southwest. Gregg was amazed by how a pool of water, right in front of him, simply evaporated within seconds.

"Have you ever seen it this dry before?" Gregg asked.

"The old ones say that it has been over one hundred years since the rains have left us for so long," David said. "That is why we have come to this place, to call to the rain."

David led Gregg along an invisible path that only he could see. They stopped at a special place—a place known to David's family and ancestors for many generations.

"There is only you, me, earth, sky, and our Creator," David said. "Today we will touch the unseen forces of this world, speaking to Mother Earth, Father Sky, and the messengers of the in-between."

"Today," he continued, "we pray rain."

David removed his shoes, turned his back, and walked toward a stone circle. Then, with his eyes closed, he did a ritual where, according to Gregg, every movement he made seemed sacred.

Once David was finished he said, "Let's go. Our work is finished here."

"Already?" Gregg asked, a bit surprised. "I thought you were going to pray for rain."

"No," David replied, "I said that I would 'pray rain.' If I had prayed *for* rain, it could never happen."

Then ...
later that afternoon ...
the "impossible" happened.

It rained.

Wait, let me correct myself. It didn't just rain.
It rained ... *hard.*

In fact, a full-fledged thunderstorm went under way.
Now ... what in the world did David do exactly?[6]

As explained in the book,
David "prayed rain" by planting the seeds of a new way:

- He began with the *feeling of gratitude* for all that is and all that has come to pass—giving thanks for the desert wind, the heat and even the drought—calling it neither good nor bad, acknowledging it as their medicine.

- Then he chose a new medicine. He *felt the feeling of what rain feels like* upon his body—all the way down to his feet—feeling the wet earth oozing between his toes.

- He *smelled the smell of rain* on the straw-and-mud walls of his village after the storms.

- He *felt what it feels like* to walk through the fields of corn growing up to his chest because the rains were so plentiful.

- He basically *felt all the feelings* of what he wished to experience.

- From that point forward, his prayer became a "prayer of thanks."

You see, faith isn't about wishing for something you don't have. And it definitely isn't about begging a distant Creator in the sky to do something for you.

Rather, real faith is about …
"feeling the feeling" that you already *do* have;
seeing what you desire in the *now*;
recognizing what you want as complete;
and with a sense of *gratitude*,
acting "as if" it's already yours.

And somehow, folks, by "honoring all possibilities," you're able to bring the ones you "choose into this world."

How can this not pump you up, right?!

○ ○ ○

The last powerful tool in creating reality is *visualization*. Try not to judge too quickly, it's not something only New Agers do. The truth is, it's something we all do. (Some of us are just not used to the word.)

Take daydreaming, for instance. Some critics find it easy to mock those who daydream often—especially when the daydreamer's goal seems so out of reach. Unfortunately, they're told by these critics to "snap out of it" or to be "realistic."

But what if daydreaming is simply a part of the process of creating? I mean, just think about it, aren't all inventions visualized in the mind first? Albert Einstein was right when he said,

"Imagination is everything.
It is the preview of life's coming attractions."

So never underestimate the power of your imagination. Who knows? Whatever you're visualizing now can change the future of the world.

○ ○ ○

Visualization can be used for a number of exercises as well—things for which many people don't even consider at all.

Research has shown that athletes who practiced visualization during rehabilitation healed significantly faster than those athletes who didn't. Another study even revealed how "visualization of muscle stretching while actually stretching increased muscle flexibility significantly."[7]

Visualization has also helped the performance of basketball players, golfers, swimmers, and even weightlifters. Name any exceptional athlete, and I'm willing to bet he or she will attribute visualization as part of their success.

Should we be surprised?
I don't think so.

Scientists have discovered that the brain can't tell the difference between what a person is imagining in the mind, and what a person is actually experiencing. So whether you're running in the mind or on an actual field—shooting basketballs through hoops in the mind or on an actual court, interestingly enough, the same areas of the brain are being activated.

o o o

There you have it.

Thoughts,
words,
feelings,
faith,
visualization—
they all work hand in hand—
benefitting you in certain ways as you learn to master them.

That being said,
you have a choice …
every …
single …
day …
to create the reality you want.

You decide whether to wake up from the alarm or to press the snooze button. You decide whether to be kind or to be a jerk. You decide whether to spend time with your family or to hang out with your friends. You decide whether to study diligently or to slack off. You decide whether to accept a sickness or to figure out a way to heal your body. You decide whether to hang out with people who bring you down or to surround yourself with people who will inspire you. You decide whether to accept what everyone else says as "truth" or to challenge the status quo when necessary. You decide whether to quit following your dream or to keep going.

You decide.

You, my friend, are a powerful force to be reckoned with.

So from this point on, as my friend, Greg Kuhn,[8] puts it:

"You're going to stop 'telling it like it is'
and start 'telling it how you want it to be.'"

'Nuff said.

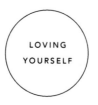

LOVING YOURSELF

EVERYTHING ELSE FLOWS FROM THERE

"Your task is not to seek for love, but merely to seek and find all the barriers within yourself that you have built against it."
Rumi

"The truth is to love yourself with the same intensity you would use to pull yourself up if you were hanging off a cliff with your fingers. As if your life depended upon it."
Kamal Ravikant

If you were to look at your body in a mirror right now, would these thoughts cross your mind?

"I'm ugly."
"I'm too fat."
"I'm too skinny."
"My ears are too big."
"My nose is too small."
"My teeth are crooked."

Now, if you were to look directly into your eyes in a mirror right now (I mean, *really* look into your eyes), what do you think you'd feel?

Pain?
Fear?
Guilt?
Worry?
Shame?
Sadness?
Insecurity?
Loneliness?

Despite all your accomplishments, what regrets do you have?

"I wish I didn't cheat on my spouse."
"I wish I didn't have so many secrets."
"I wish I were a better husband (or wife)."
"I wish I were a better father (or mother)."
"I wish I could provide better for my family."

Now, let me be straight up with you for a moment. I want you to be completely honest when answering this next question, too. No bullshit. Don't give an answer you think I (or anyone else) would wanna hear. Just be totally transparent. That's all I'm asking. OK, are you ready?

Do you love yourself?

I'm not talking about being some narcissistic, arrogant prick here.

I'm talking about *really* loving yourself.

If you're not exactly sure what that looks like,
here are a couple of things to think about:

- Do you feel worthy of love?
- Do you have a healthy regard for yourself?
- Do you do the things which make you happy?
- Do you no longer say bad things about yourself?
- Do you no longer wish you were somebody else?
- Do you no longer feel the need to judge others unfairly?
- Do you nurture yourself physically, mentally and emotionally?

- Do you treat yourself as though you were your own best friend?

- Do you no longer feel the need to compare yourself with others?

- Do you acknowledge your potential and believe in your abilities?

- Do you accept yourself no matter how many mistakes you've made?

If you answered *yes* to any of these questions, then you're definitely on the road to loving yourself. But if you answered a big, fat *NO* to any of these (and don't be too hard on yourself either), well then, the fact that you're acknowledging it is already a good place to start.

Sure, we've all had our "bad" days here and there. I'll admit, even I've had moments where I've lost sight of my own self-worth. But I think the goal for all of us is to regain focus and start loving ourselves again.

Now you might be wondering why I'm not immediately jumping into all the fun and amazing stories about healing, money and success, right? Well, although those topics are important, I believe the issue of loving yourself is even more important. *In fact, I think it's the most important message of this entire book.*

Think about it. You can have all the health, wealth and success in the world—you could even have a bunch of people *like* you …

but if *you* don't love yourself,
then what else really matters?

○ ○ ○

As a child, it was very hard for me to love myself. Being born with a deformed right hand, I became extremely self-conscious about it. I know it can sound trivial to some folks, but to be honest, it wasn't for *me*. In fact, it seemed like my whole world revolved around this issue I had with it—not because it was inevitable, but because I consciously chose to think a certain way.

Growing up, I was teased a lot by other kids. I even got bullied here and there. Whether it was kids in the neighborhood or classmates at school, I felt I constantly had something that made me an easy target for them. With disgusted looks on their faces, they'd usually say something like, "At least I don't have one hand!"

I wish I could say I never let their words nor the nasty looks on their faces get to me. But truthfully, they did—in more ways than I would've liked.

Year after year, my self-esteem only sunk lower and lower. I didn't just suffer from self-rejection, it was my cocoon. And for the longest time, what I didn't have got in the way of me seeing all that I already was.

I was headed down the painful path of not loving myself.

I felt ...
ugly,
different,
and insecure.

"No girl's ever going to like me."
"What kind of job will I have in the future?"
"Will I deal with uncomfortable stares for the rest of my life?"

These were the fears I had on a daily basis.

And because I had such a hard time accepting myself, I ended up either keeping my right hand in my pocket most of the time, or hiding it under the sleeve of my sweater. I hardly ever took it out for others to see. I was just too afraid to see people's reactions.

Whenever I did *try* taking my hand out of my pocket in public, it felt so unnatural to me. And it also *felt* like the whole world was looking at me as though I were some sort of freak show.

Yup, my fear was seriously *that* bad.

In fact, my fear was so bad to the point that, even in my early twenties, when my job required me to do a lot of public speaking, I still kept my hand in my pocket the entire time I spoke in front of a crowd.

(Note: you're gonna have to remember this particular struggle of mine in order for the end of the book to make any sense. So don't forget it.)

○ ○ ○

As I mentioned in an earlier chapter, I also grew up very religious. Well, to be more specific, I grew up learning fear-based teachings disguised as "love." My view of God was schizophrenic. For instance, I was taught that God loves me whenever I do something good—but in a split second—this "loving" God supposedly gets "super pissed off" with me whenever I do something "bad." This inevitably made my "relationship" between this deity and I very unstable. It was so stinkin' confusing. (To read more about my religious journey, you can check out my previous book *So You Thought You Knew*.)

To make matters worse, this same fear-based religion also taught me to have a very low view of who I *was* at the time.

For example, I was constantly told by others that my heart is wicked and deceitful. That it is "never about me" but "all about God." If I had an accomplishment, I was always encouraged to say "It's not me, it's God" because God had to "get all the glory." This seriously made it awkward for me to say "Thank you" at times because I'd supposedly be "taking the credit away from God."

I guess I shouldn't be surprised.

After all, I was taught that I was nothing but a …
"filthy,
depraved,
unworthy,
wretched sinner."

Looking back, I now realize how damaging this view of myself has been. Dude, just think about it. As a parent, can you imagine walking into your daughter's bedroom one day, and as you're entering through the door, you hear her crying to God saying, "I'm nothing. I'm filthy. I'm a dirty sinner." (Wow, what a way to build a child's self-esteem.) What do you think is gonna happen to your daughter once she starts *identifying* with those labels?

Do you think she'll grow up to be a positive and confident woman who knows her value? Do you think she'll have a healthy sense of self-worth and respect for herself?

I doubt it.

Remember, "we become what we think about."

o o o

What about you? What was your story growing up? Did your

parents say unloving things to you like ...
"you're so stupid" or ...
"I wish you were never born!" or ...
"you'll never be like so-and-so" or ...
"you'll never amount to anything"?

Did your parents neglect you 'cause they were too busy partying? Or maybe you screwed up so bad in the past and now they want nothing to do with you. Or maybe you were raised by great parents who did love you, but for some reason, you've always had a hard time believing it. Or maybe you've never even met your parents.

Whatever your experience has been, everyone has their own story.

It's interesting because we see people every single day—everywhere we go—yet we have no idea what the heck is going on in their minds. Some could even look like the happiest people in the world, but deep down, they're hurting ... *badly* ... even to the point of wanting to commit suicide. And sadly, without us even knowing it, our faces might actually be the last thing they see before they end their lives.

That being the case, despite how "perfect" someone can look on the outside, we all hurt at different times and for different reasons. We all go through crap sometimes that, honestly, we just don't wanna talk about. So what do we end up doing to save face or to keep ourselves from being a burden to others?

We keep the hurt inside.
We pretend to look OK to others.
We appear to "have it altogether."

The question is …

Do we love ourselves?

○ ○ ○

Society has told us what to believe, how to look, what to eat, what to wear, what kind of car to drive, and what kind of electronic devices we should own. And without us even knowing it, we've been living off the beliefs (and possibly lies) of other people. In a sense, we've allowed society (specifically the media) to create us.

This is where the *ego* comes in—and I'm not simply referring to someone with a big head who thinks he or she's "all that." I'm talking about our collective thoughts and beliefs which we identify with as being distinctly us.

For example, in our mind we hear things like "you're supposed to be this" and "you're supposed to be that" and "you're supposed to be blah, blah, blah." Then we start identifying with all those things we're '"supposed to be" and—wanting to find fulfillment—end up creating a *false self*—thinking it's us, when in reality, it's not.

Then once we start identifying with our "false self," we end up wrestling with our brokenness, our emptiness, and our pain. And of course we'd wish these experiences would all go away in an instant, right? So what do some of us pursue in order to "fix" ourselves?

Money.
Sex.
Power.

Later to realize that they make us feel even …
more brokenness,
more emptiness,
and *more* pain.

Why?

Are these things bad in and of themselves? Of course not. But to think these things can heal, fill, or make us complete—well, we'd be fooling ourselves, that's for sure.

What it comes down to is this: *Why do you do what you do?*

There's an important distinction to be made here.

You see, *context* and *motivation* is everything.

Are your pursuits *stemming* from self-love,
or are they ways for you to try to *attain* love?

Big difference.

'Cause if your pursuits for pleasures in this life are only to feed the ego without having genuine self-love first, then watch out for the person you end up *becoming*. And don't be surprised if others end up not liking you either.

So let me ask you this again.

Do you love yourself?

○ ○ ○

"But Josh," you might say, "you have no idea how many messed up things I've done in my life. Why should I love myself?"

First of all, I don't need to know what you've done. And second, I'm not gonna get on some high horse and compare myself to you. Trust me, we've all done stupid things we wish we didn't do.

Now hear me out on this. OK, so you might've done some pretty shady things in the past. I get that. But here's the thing, you still gotta come to a place where you accept what's already happened and "own it," so to speak.

What's done is done.

Keep your head up.
Learn from your mistakes.
And realize your future doesn't have to be like your past.

And you … and I really mean this … gotta move on.

For goodness sake, enough with all the self-loathing. Stop feeling the need to beat yourself up all the time. It's pointless. It'll only keep you down. And trust me, that's not where you wanna stay.

You're better than that.

The truth is, despite your mistakes, your failures, your shortcomings … none of them define you … at all. They never have. They never will. 'Cause you are *not* your negative actions. So stop focusing on them.

On the flip-side, stop focusing and *trying so hard* to be a good person, too. I know that sounds weird, but I'm being serious. The more you focus on *trying* to become good, the more guilt you're gonna experience once you fail to live up to your expectations.

Receive the insight given by Eckhart Tolle where he says,

"You don't become good by trying to be good,
but by finding the goodness that is already within you,
and allowing that goodness to emerge."

You see, it's not about trying to become what you're supposed to be. It's about *waking up* to the reality of what you already are and seeing everything else flow from there.

Then once you recognize your inherent goodness, here's what you need to do concerning your past mistakes:

Forgive yourself.

Take in a deep breath …
and take all your hidden guilt …
and just …
let …
it …
go.

Not later. Not tomorrow. Now.

Look, life forgives you when you make mistakes, doesn't ? For instance, let's say you fall and scrape your knee or burn your hand from touching a hot stove. What happens afterward?

You form new skin.

Life takes what's wrong and makes it right again. In other words, it *naturally* gives your body a second chance.

Since life forgives and restores your body without rubbing it in by saying, "You idiot! I told you not to do that!," then why can't you forgive yourself and believe your mistakes can somehow be redeemed?

It's *never* too late to have a fresh start.

The past is the past. It's time to give yourself another chance. Speaking of second chances, what comes to mind are the stories of those who've attempted suicide by jumping off the Golden Gate Bridge in San Francisco. Prior to jumping, many of them felt depressed and hopeless, looking for a way out to escape the pain of life.

But after they jumped, here's what several survivors admitted:

They regretted their decision in midair.

One survivor, Ken Baldwin, concerning his jump said, "I instantly realized that everything in my life that I'd thought was unfixable was totally fixable—except for having just jumped."

Another survivor, Kevin Hines, said about the time he was in flight, "My first thought was *What the hell did I just do? I don't want to die.*"[1]

You see, they didn't wanna end their *lives*.

They only wanted to end their *pain*.

And some of them,
according to their friends and family,
simply wanted to be *loved*.[2]

Why?

'Cause in these cases, their lives depended upon it.

○ ○ ○

Once you begin loving yourself, it's interesting to notice how life suddenly starts loving you back. I'm not saying it's gonna be perfect, but you'll be surprised to see less friction in the world around you. Things will begin to flow, so to speak, where circumstances magically begin working in your favor for a change.

You'll also start catching things you like about yourself. You'll start noticing the positives more than the negatives. You'll begin appreciating just how special you really are.

Think about it.

You are you.

And there's no one else *exactly* like you.
How amazing is that?!

You are a gift to the world.

And, like with any gift, what's *inside* is ultimately what matters.

○ ○ ○

Finally, let me share something I found in Kamal Ravikant's bestselling book *Love Yourself.* It's a simple exercise, but sometimes the simplest things are the most powerful.

Here are the steps:

Step one: Set a timer for five minutes.
Step two: Stand in front of a mirror. Relax. Breathe.
Step three: Look into your eyes. Focus on your left eye.
Step four: Look into your left eye, say, "I love myself."
Step five: Gently repeat "I love myself."

As Kamal says in the book,

"If anyone ever looked in your eyes, knowing that you love them, this is what they saw. Give yourself the same gift."

And why is it a gift?

Because …

loving yourself …

changes …

everything.

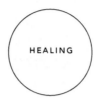

HEALING

LIVING NATURALLY "SUPERNATURAL"

"What makes you sick, is everything you are not.
What makes you well, is everything that you are."
Ramtha

"Miracles do not happen in contradiction to nature,
but only in contradiction to what is known in nature."
St. Augustine

It was 2005—a birthday party. The music was playing and it was time for us to "get our boogie on" (wait, do people still say that?) on the dance floor. Some people formed a circle and, before I knew it, I started breakdancing, challenging some random guy across from me to a "battle," which is basically when two or more dancers square off. All I wanted to do was to have some fun and show off my latest moves.

After I did my "mini performance" on the ground, I got up. But there was a problem: I couldn't *stay* up. All of a sudden, I got numb below my waist and went straight back down on the ground—but this time, I wasn't dancing. I wasn't sure what was happening to my legs. And I started feeling excruciating pain shooting through my back. *What the hell is going on?* I thought. *I didn't even slam my back on the ground or anything like that!*

The other breakdancer responded to my challenge—"busting out" his moves for all to see—having no clue at all what was happening to me. And me, well, I just stayed on the ground. There was no way in hell I was gonna get back into the dance circle. Trust me, trying to win a friendly dance battle was the last thing on my mind.

That night I drove home in a lot of pain.

The good news: I was still alive.
The bad news: I had a herniated disc and suffered from sciatica.

(The disc in between the vertebrae of my spine was being

crushed and slipping out—pinching a nerve. This caused a sharp pain to travel from my back, through my butt, all the way down to my leg.)

The pain I experienced was bad. No, no, no, it was *really* bad.

Whenever I got out of bed in the morning, it felt like I was stepping on dozens of needles as soon as my feet touched the floor.

As for my body.
Whenever I coughed, it hurt.
Whenever I sneezed, it hurt.
Whenever I laughed, it hurt.

As for everyday challenges.
I couldn't sit for too long.
I walked slower than a turtle.
I would randomly fall while walking.
I had to hold onto rails walking up and down the stairs.

As for trying to get better.
I slept sideways with a pillow between my legs.
I did stretches all throughout the day.
I took pain killers regularly.
I tried physical therapy.
I tried acupuncture.

Surprisingly, throughout the months that followed,
my situation only got worse.

I cried myself to sleep for many nights. In fact, some of my biggest fears were that, if I were to have children, I'd never be able to carry them because of the pressure it would put on my back. Or that I'd never be capable of being physically active again—things like running or playing sports. Or worse yet, I'd never be able to walk normally ever again.

I remember thinking, "Man, it's one thing for me to not be able to dance anymore (which I loved to do), but now I can hardly walk."

But this was only the beginning of some major problems.

o o o

Not too long after, I found myself over at a friend's house for dinner. Later that evening, I started to feel severe pain in my chest and on the left side of my body, so I took a rest on the couch for a while. Once I got up around midnight, I decided to head straight home.

Shortly after I arrived home, I started freaking out the second I was alone in my bedroom. I thought I was having a heart attack. And I thought I was gonna die right then and there. I wanted to go to the hospital but I didn't have health insurance at the time. I didn't know what to do. It probably wasn't the smartest move, but I ended up staying home and forcing myself to endure the pain until I fell asleep.

The good news: I woke up the next day.

The bad news: I suffered from Gastroesophageal reflux disease (GERD).

(What caused me to have this painful experience? Stress? Overeating? Fatty foods? All of the above? One thing's for sure, I never suffered from any severe chest pain or heartburn my entire life until that night.)

Ever since the first scare at my friend's house, I literally had pain in my chest every single day, strong heartburn, and the disgusting taste of vomit in my throat from that day forward.

Lifestyle changes.
I took medicine daily.
I couldn't eat all the food I loved.
I ate what was considered to be "healthy" food.
I slept with my head elevated on two pillows to keep the acid down.

I did absolutely everything I could think of to get better. Unfortunately, just like my back problems, I got worse. There I was, in my early twenties, already suffering from back *and* throat problems.

It was the most challenging time in my life—both physically and emotionally. But all the suffering and questioning led me on a journey to discover what I, thankfully, now know today.

OK, fast-forward several years to today.

At this time of writing, I'm now 33 years old.
I've hardly had any back pain since.
And I literally eat whatever I want now, without any problems.

(I still get emotional just thinking about my healing though.)

So what exactly happened to me?

Well, a lot happened! In fact, I could write an entire book about it. (Sounds like a good idea, huh?) But in this book, I'm gonna spare you the autobiographical details. Instead, I wanna go straight into some of the things I learned about healing.

o o o

In this chapter, I wanna give my readers a measure of *responsibility*. (Don't let that word scare you.) But first, before I get into that, let me give my general thoughts about healing.

The principles of healing are woven into the very fabric of the universe and are available to anyone, anytime, and anywhere. The ability to heal doesn't belong to just one group, religion, sect, or even to one "special" person.

In other words, healing is available to *all*—there's no favoritism.

Being involved for several years in what's considered "miraculous" healing, I'm well aware of the different healing modalities out there which are found throughout the world. I'm also aware that, while there are some healing practitioners who share their technique's success—some are even bold enough to claim that their technique is the *only* one that's valid.

But the fact of the matter is,
the universal power to heal resides in *every* human being.

But go ahead, stick to whatever method you want, for all I care. If it works for you, then great.

For me, however,
the only thing that matters is if you exercise this:

Faith.

The way I see it, faith is the necessary component when it comes to healing—irrespective of the modality you use. If you exercise faith using a particular technique of your choosing, I believe it'll work for you—no matter how simple or complicated it is.

You see, with faith you can accomplish anything. So take heart. No matter what kind of unwanted symptoms you have appearing in your body right now, you can bring about change.

But here's the thing: *it all starts from the inside out.*

o o o

Is it safe to say—*at least to some degree*—
that your body is a product of your thoughts?

Does your body speak the language of your mind?

Think about it. Even in medical science, people are beginning to see the connection between the mind and the body. The two are, in fact, intertwined. The connection is so real that some conclude our beliefs *determine* the function of our body—that is to say, they have the capacity to make us sick or make us well.

I know some people may find this hard to swallow and say, "I would never think my body into making it sick."

Of course you wouldn't—at least not *consciously*. But as I mentioned before, you're mostly controlled by your subconscious mind. So whether or not you consciously want to be sick, it doesn't matter. What matters is whether or not your subconscious mind is thinking "sickly" thoughts.

According to Dr. Bruce Lipton, a highly respected cellular biologist, illness and disease are caused by *stress* at least 95% of the time. That's a pretty high percentage, don't you think?

So now the question is, *Where does stress actually begin?*

You got it, stress begins in the mind.

For instance, one negative thought leads to another negative thought … which can then lead to what's considered a "disease."[1] You see, although there are bunch of "diseases" out there, there's a pretty good chance the cause was stress to begin with.

Bitterness, unforgiveness, self-hatred, etc.—these are all no-nos for us to keep inside. They definitely have an effect on our bodies. Sure, they might not manifest into an obvious sickness immediately, but they can create a chain of negativity which can then lead to sickness.

I mean, think about it—high blood pressure, inflammation, acne, pain, they don't just spring up out of nowhere. There's a cause-and-effect going on where thoughts eventually become a biological fact. This is why it's so important for us to change our negative thoughts into positive thoughts before they snowball into something destructive.

As a matter of fact, self-help guru Louise Hay believes all sickness is due to wrong thinking—reflecting a person's internal state. In other words, whatever you believe *internally*, you'll manifest *externally*. As the saying goes, "As within, so without. " Now, whether or not you agree with her completely, there does seem to be at least some truth to it.[2]

And Louise isn't alone in her thinking either. Lissa Rankin, author of *Mind Over Medicine* says, "Change your thoughts, change your behaviors. Change your behaviors, change your biochemistry." As a physician, she "gets it." "It's not some New Age metaphysical thing," she says, "it's simple physiology."[3]

So how can anyone believe our thoughts don't matter?

o o o

Someone can protest,
"No, no, no! It's all genetics!"

We've all heard it before, haven't we? If someone in your family suffers from something like diabetes or cancer, well, guess what?—*you* are supposedly next.

Genes, as we've been told, are our destiny.

Well, that is the *traditional* view. But according to a relatively new field of study, there's a new bad boy (or should I say "good boy") in town.

It's called ... *epigenetics*.

I first learned about epigenetics several years ago when I read Bruce Lipton's book *The Biology of Belief*.

Let me break it down for you as simply as I can.

The word "epigenetics" literally means "control above genetics"—meaning, other influences can modify the genetic code without actually changing the DNA.[4]

Here's an experiment Bruce did which explains this even further:

He took one single stem cell and placed it in a petri dish.
The single stem cell divided every ten hours.
After a week there were more than 50,000 cells in the dish.
He split up the cells and placed them into three different culture dishes.
Each culture dish had a distinct "environment."

Now here's where it gets interesting.

In one dish, the cells formed *muscle*.
In the second dish, the cells formed *bone*.
In the third dish, the cells formed *fat*.

Wait a minute … muscle, bone and fat? But weren't all the cells *genetically identical*? So how in the world did that happen?

The answer: *environment*.

You see, when the cells were exposed to a "good" environment, the cells stayed healthy. But when the cells were exposed to a "bad" environment, the cells got sick. But that's not all. If you were to take the cells from a bad environment and place them in a good environment, then, voilà!—they *naturally* recover!

Remember:
Good environment = healthy cells.
Bad environment = sick cells.

Why is this so important?

Well, according to Bruce, a human is like a "skin-covered" petri dish containing 50 trillion cells. And guess what has the power to the change the cellular environment? (It shouldn't be too hard to figure this one out by now.)

Once again, the *mind*.

How exactly does your mind change the cellular environment?

Get this—it's based on how your mind *interprets* life events.

For instance, if you open your eyes and see (interpret) love in your world, it causes the brain to release positive chemicals like dopamine and oxytocin into the blood. This interpretation of the world leads to healthy growth.

But, if you open your eyes and see (interpret) fear in your world, it causes the brain to release stress hormones and inflammatory agents into the blood. This interpretation of the world negatively affects the growth of cells and can even cause them to die.[5]

So what does epigenetics tell us again?

- Interpretation (perception) is everything.
- You are not a victim of your genes.
- You control your destiny.

(Did you just read those last three lines?!)

○ ○ ○

I'll never forget a book I read by Anita Moorjani called *Dying to Be Me*. It actually confirmed a lot of what I was already learning at the time about the mind/body connection.

(WARNING: SPOILER ALERT)

In the book, Anita shares her story of how she suffered from cancer, had a near-death-experience, and was what many would consider, miraculously healed. Anita said that, after experiencing her miracle, she's often asked how she got cancer in the first place.

Her simple and straightforward answer remains the same: *fear*.

Anita's answer isn't surprising when you think about it. I mean, two people in her life both died from cancer. So, of course, she automatically assumed she was next in line. That being said, Anita ended up being afraid of just about everything—the feeling of being disliked, letting people down, not being good enough, illness, cancer, dying, and even living. She also started to believe that "everything created cancer—pesticides, microwaves, preservatives, genetically modified foods, sunshine, air pollution, plastic food containers, mobile phones, and so on."

Obviously, Anita's interpretation of her world was predominantly based on fear. And since thoughts become things, she ended up getting the very thing she feared the most—the "C" word—cancer.

Fortunately, there was a turning-point for Anita. She spent some time in India with a yoga master hoping it would help her deal with the cancer. Ironically, (to her at least) the yoga master didn't even believe she had cancer. So she tried convincing him by mentioning how medical doctors conducted tests and diagnosed her with lymphoma.

I love the yoga master's response to her "proof":

> "*Cancer* is just a word that creates fear. Forget about that word, and let's just focus on balancing your body. All illnesses are just symptoms of imbalance. No illness can remain when your entire system is in balance."

Thankfully, she took the yoga master at his word, and after her shift in thinking, she started to get better—both physically and emotionally. But when she went back home to Hong Kong, well-meaning people in her life instilled doubts concerning the methods she learned in India, and her road to healing ended up being short-lived. Her fear returned, and to no surprise, her health started to deteriorate all over again.

o o o

As for myself, when I first heard I was diagnosed with GERD several years ago, I decided to learn everything I could about it. I did what a lot of people do when they first experience painful symptoms. I "googled" it on the internet. I read books on it. Thing is, rather than giving me hope and comfort, the information I learned actually scared the crap out of me even more!

I remember late one evening—right before midnight—I began reading a book on GERD. The book had photos of what it actually looks like inside a person's body who suffers from the "disease." Once I saw one of the images, I thought, "Is that what it looks like inside me?"

I immediately put the book down and started jogging outside my parent's condo till early morning—hoping the exercise would improve my health somehow.

But as I ran, nothing but fear continued to dominate my mind.

o o o

I can understand why you'd wanna learn more about a "condition" in order to get better, but without the proper mindset, it can actually work against you. Believe it or not, focusing on an illness won't just make you more sick, it can actually *keep you sick*, too.

How?

'Cause what you focus on expands. It's all about *directed* energy. That's why I don't encourage people to go around constantly telling people how sick they are. With enough focused attention (and emotion), it'll back-fire on them.

Remember how powerful words were in Masaru Emoto's water experiment?

Be careful not to say things like:

"I'm always sick."
"I'm allergic to that."
"I'm gonna die in six months."

"I can't get better."
"I can't lose weight."
"I can't do anything about my condition."

"I'll get arthritis when I'm old."
"I'll lose my hearing when I'm old."
"I'll lose my eyesight when I'm old."

Remember, every "I am" or "I can't" or "I will" is a *creation*.

You. Get. What. You. Believe.

So choose your thoughts and words wisely.

o o o

Am I saying you should never go see a doctor and/or take medicine? Nope, that's not what I'm saying at all. But there are some things to consider.

There's an awesome book by Norman Cousins called *Anatomy of an Illness* which has been mentioned in major medical journals around the world. In it, he shares how he suffered from an "incurable" degenerative disease called ankylosing spondylitis. And according to the "experts," his chances of full recovery were very slim.

To make a long story short,
he's known as the patient who ...
laughed his way to health.

Several key things were instrumental to his recovery:

- Accepting responsibility
- A supportive partnership with his doctor
- Laughter (watching funny movies)
- Happiness (reading his favorite comic books)
- A will to live

What stood out to me the most in Norman's story was the importance of a doctor's role in a patient's recovery. In a way, they can be seen as a type of placebo. You see, in general, people do tend to "take the word" of those in authority (e.g., doctors, scientists, priests), don't they? It's understandable.

But here's the problem, what if the "experts" are wrong?

For one thing, if a doctor says your condition is "incurable" or "terminal" or "that you only have six months to live," those words can be very powerful to you as a patient and can greatly affect your subconscious mind—depending on how much weight you give them, of course.

But based on how the mind works,
even if the doctor is wrong,
your *belief* in the doctor ...
will make the doctor's words a reality.

o o o

Did you know that countless people are healed when given placebos? If you're not that familiar with what they are, they're basically a kind of imitation medicine which can be found in the form of either a sugar pill or even a saline injection. In themselves, they don't do jack squat, but the patient doesn't know that. In fact, the patient doesn't even have to know because healing doesn't come from the pill itself.

Instead, healing occurs because of the *patient's faith in the pill.*

That, my friend, is how the placebo effect works..

The placebo effect can be used during surgery as well. Consider the study published by an orthopedic surgeon named Bruce Mosley. He documented a case where ten men needed knee surgery. Five of these men received the *actual* surgery, while the other five received a *fake (or placebo) surgery.* Those who received the fake surgery had their skin sliced open and were sewn back up again with no medical procedure whatsoever.

The surprising results:
all ten men had greater mobility and less pain.

Not only that, those who had the fake surgery did just as well as those who had the real operations! And in other cases I've read, sometimes the placebo surgeries were more successful than the real surgeries themselves!

Ever hear the story of a group of eight men in their 70s and 80s who, when pretending to be 22 years younger, literally became "physiologically younger"—both "structurally as well as functionally"?

Or what about the story during World War II where a nurse injected a "badly wounded soldier" with saline (salt water) because morphine was in short supply. Surprisingly, the soldier reacted as though he'd received the actual drug! *(If I was the nurse at the time and saw the soldier react the way he did, I'd probably laugh in my mind and be like, "Are you serious, dude?!)*

Talk about the power of the mind![6]

So based on these examples, yes, the placebo effect does work. But things also work the other way around with something called the *nocebo effect*. You see, while the placebo effect shows the power of positive belief to help and heal you, the nocebo effect displays the power of negative belief to hurt or even kill you.

For instance, a patient is told that a certain treatment can cause vomiting, nausea, headaches, hair loss, etc. Then guess what happens after the treatment? They end up suffering the very things they're told to expect—not because the treatment actually induces these effects, but because the patient *believes* what they're told. This has been evidenced in certain control group studies.

I'm also reminded of spiritual teacher, Deepak Chopra, whose friend died by the ultimate nocebo response—a modern day "voodoo death"—if you wanna call it that. As the story goes, Deepak's friend found out he had a black mark on his lung (which meant lung cancer), and within three weeks, he died. One day, when his office was being cleaned out, X-rays taken of him from *twenty years* prior were found. And guess what was on those X-rays?—*the same black mark on his lung!* In other words, once Deepak's friend found out about the black spot on his lung, it possibly triggered a negative belief and his mind simply took over from there.[7]

You see, there's a big difference between ...
dying *with* lung "cancer,"
and dying *from* lung "cancer."[8]

This is why I get so turned off by the many prescription drug ads I see running on television and the internet. It's like there's a pill for every single ailment out there. The thing is, not only will these drugs supposedly give you relief, but they can, through the power of the nocebo effect, also *create* new ailments based on your acceptance of the warnings on the labels. It's stinkin' crazy.

o o o

It's one thing for your beliefs to heal your own body, but it's also possible for your beliefs to heal *other* people's bodies as well.

I remember listening to Gregg Braden talk about a tumor disappearing from a woman's bladder in less than three minutes. This insanely-fast healing took place in Beijing, China at … get this … a *medicineless hospital!* (No, that wasn't a typo.)

Here's what happened in the actual healing video:

- Through the use of a sonogram, there was a split screen—one still image of the woman's cancer (left side), and another image of the "cancer" in "real time" (right side).

- Next to the lady were three practitioners who were trained to "feel the feeling" of healing on her behalf.

- The practitioners start chanting a word over and over again.

And then …

BAM!

Cancer disappears … in less than three minutes!

So what was the *word* the practitioners were chanting?

According to Gregg, the word … "loosely translated, means 'already happened … it's already done.'"

There wasn't any magic in the word(s)—just like how I mentioned there isn't any magic in techniques. In fact, the practitioners could've used any word(s) if they wanted to.

What mattered most was—with whatever word(s) they used—they *created the feeling* that the healing had *already* taken place.

"Not that it's [healing] going to happen," Gregg says,
"and not that it's about to happen,"
but "that it has already happened."

This is the power of believing.

This is the power of what I've been calling *faith* throughout the book.

○ ○ ○

Are you suffering from any sickness or disability?

Well, you have a choice.

You can either accept and live with it.
Or you can be like, "Heck no! I'm tired of this!"

If you wanna try healing your body, here are some concluding tips you can try:

1. Release all emotional negativity in your life (e.g., unforgiveness, bitterness, anger). Take all that crap and *let them all go.*

2. Have an "attitude of gratitude." Be thankful for your health now. Don't wait till Thanksgiving.

3. Keep your thoughts positive on life, health and love. Don't focus on your "disease"—you'll only be sustaining it.

4. If you believe in the power of prayer, instead of praying "for" healing, think of prayer as an *awareness* of healing.

5. Practice *autosuggestion* daily. Sometimes there can be a conflict between your two minds. For example, your conscious mind says "I'm healed," but your subconscious mind says "I'm sick." You'll notice it if you feel like you're lying to yourself. To ease the tension, change it up a bit. Instead, you can say, "Everyday, in *every way*, I'm getting healthier and healthier" if it helps. The goal is to bring harmony between the two minds.[9]

6. Set aside time to visualize yourself completely healed. See yourself doing "what you're not supposed to be doing." For example, if your leg is injured, see yourself running ... fast! See rays of light flowing all throughout your body, repairing the damaged area(s). And make your visions so vivid where you see colors and hear sounds.

Use your sense of smell—your sense of touch (it's all about detail)—but most of all, *feel the reality* of it all.

7. Listen to healing affirmation audio recordings when going to bed. Remember, being in a drowsy state allows your mind to be more receptive and less likely to argue back with your conscious doubts. In other words, when your mind is in what's called a theta (hypnotic) state, it's easier for it to download the suggestions said to it.

8. Laugh, and laugh, and laugh, and laugh. It's the best medicine after all, right? Remember, part of staying healthy actually involves not taking life too seriously.

9. "Act as if" you're already healthy. It can create the feeling you're wanting which then leads to manifesting.

10. Whatever you decide to do, don't give up.

○ ○ ○

Let me end this chapter with a story about the legendary badass, Bruce Lee. Not only did he kick butt in his action-packed movies, but he also kicked a major setback out of his life.

For those who don't know, Bruce suffered from a serious back injury during his career. He was even told he'd never participate in martial arts ever again. But, being the determined person he was, he didn't give up.

Bruce turned to self-help books for inspiration.
Wrote the phrase "Walk on" on the back of his business card.
And bought a special stand for the card and kept it on his desk. (The card was a constant reminder for him to keep moving forward.)

Through the ordeal, Bruce eventually worked himself into the best shape of his life and even developed an art called *Jeet Kune Do.*

You know the saying "where there's a will there's a way"? Well, Bruce Lee totally lived up to it.

And now I'm telling you …
don't give up.
See yourself well.
Feel yourself well.
Take action.

And "walk on."

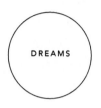

DREAMS

JUMP. FALL.
FLY.

"Whether you think you can, or you think you can't—
you're right."
Henry Ford

"Now, if you know what you're worth,
then go out and get what you're worth."
Rocky Balboa

In 2008 I decided to take a leap of faith (at least for me it was). It was a time in my life when a lot of exciting things were already happening. I was constantly on-the-go—speaking at different events, networking, and meeting a bunch of people. And if those weren't enough, I was also one semester shy of finishing up my master's degree program.

As one who is always open to learn, it was a time in my life when a lot of my views about God, healing, love, faith—pretty much life in general—started to radically change. And it's not because I planned it either. It's because I started listening more to the voice within.

There was a passion in me … a fire … a determination … of wanting to share what I've learned with the rest of the world. You see, for several years, I had been able to help people break free from fear-based religion by sharing inspiring and thought-provoking talks across the country.

But this time around, my dream was to take these talks abroad.

The Philippines ended up becoming impressed upon my heart somehow. I started envisioning myself living there, making a positive impact in people's lives by building relationships and doing talks throughout the nation. The thing is though, I hardly knew anyone there.

But this desire I had wouldn't go away.
In fact, it only grew stronger over time.

I eventually told my friends and family about my dream 'cause I wanted feedback ... advice ... counsel—anything to help me with my decision. While everyone was pretty much supportive, at the same time, some of them had genuine concerns.

For instance, I was reminded of how my "life was going to be different," how I already had it "pretty good" right here in America, and how I might even struggle there financially if I were to go. Now, no one flat-out told me not to go. But the message I often got was that my comfortable life in the U.S. wasn't going to be so "comfortable" in this third world country.

But.

I'll never forget the day I made my decision to move to the Philippines indefinitely. It was the month of August, 2008 and to be honest, it kind of "just happened." I'm serious. I don't know how else to put it.

Here's the story:

One day I was at school responding to emails on the library computer. A fellow student approached me and we started chatting about what we'd been up to. Then, for some strange reason, in the middle of our "small talk," I blurted out, "I'm going to the Philippines."

Yup, just like that.

The words came out of my mouth unexpectedly. I dunno why.

After exiting the library I ran into another friend of mine. The same thing happened again. During our "small talk," I blurted out that I was moving to the Philippines. I actually caught myself thinking, *Why do I keep saying that?* And then I said it again, and again, and again—to different people—all throughout the day.

I'll admit, the reactions from people got me excited to go—solidifying my decision even more. I started thinking, "Oh man, I guess I'm really gonna do this."

Once I started planning for the big move, I realized I wanted to leave a lot sooner than I'd thought—the end of the semester to be exact (December 2008). Problem was, I thought I had one more semester left in order to graduate.

Should I forget about graduating and just go? But I already spent so much money on my education. Who needs a degree anyway? I've been doing what I love (traveling and speaking) without it. These thoughts and questions kept running through my mind.

Then the unexpected happened—a *good* mistake—which actually ended up working in my favor. I later realized I miscalculated the units I needed in order to graduate. The whole time I thought I was gonna graduate the following year in the Spring of 2009. But no, after fixing my mistake, I realized I was gonna graduate at the end of the 2008 school year!—around the time I planned to leave for the Philippines!

Things were falling into place.

One day, a millionaire eventually heard about my desire to leave for the Philippines and invited me to his office for a visit. I honestly didn't know what to expect. I mean, I hardly knew the guy. At the time, all I knew was that he had attended one of my public talks and liked it. So I assumed the invite might've had something to do with that. I couldn't have been more wrong, considering what happened next.

That afternoon in his office, one of the first things he asked me was, "So, tell me, why do you want to go to the Philippines?"

I didn't think too much of it at the time. I simply began sharing my heart and telling him about my dream.

When he asked me where I was gonna stay in the Philippines, here's how the rest of the conversation went:

"But I'm not sure where I'm gonna live though."
"Don't worry about it."
"What?" (I was so confused.)
"I said 'don't worry about it.' I'm gonna pay your rent for a few years."
"What?" (I was still confused.)
"Don't be surprised, Josh. God is full of surprises."

No joke ... at that moment ... I froze—completely shocked with what I'd just heard. Then, in an instant, my eyes got super watery. Tears started to run down my face. I was so overwhelmed, I was rendered speechless. *Is this really happening?* I thought.

A few weeks passed and I realized I had enough money in my bank account to last me a couple of months in the Philippines. I thought, *Hmm ... I still have a car. I can sell it off to make more money.* Since it was still in good condition, I could've sold it for at least $10,000. And when you think about it, if that amount were to be converted into pesos, well, I think I'd be off to a pretty good financial start.

But then this crazy idea kicked in. I thought, *Nah, that's too easy. I wanna challenge myself. I wanna see money come to me in miraculous ways. So many good (and unexpected) things have been happening to me anyway. Why not expect more?*

So what did I do with my car? I dumped it in the ocean. Just kidding! I ended up giving it away to my sister for free.

Months went by, and one thing after another kept confirming my decision to go. (At least that's what I felt was happening.) I kept following the "signs," so to speak—believing everything would fall into place. And you know what? They definitely were. (Looking back, I now realize I was creating my dream, shaping my life into a new reality.)

The desire within grew even stronger.
I didn't just *want to* move to the Philippines anymore.
Now it felt like I *had to* move to the Philippines.

December came along and I graduated with a master's degree. January followed and I had this big "going away" party with a bunch of my friends and family. And the day of my departure inched closer.

Nothing could stop me now.

But as my departure drew near, I began to have mixed emotions. You see, on the one hand, I got super excited just thinking about moving to another country. Yet on the other hand, it wasn't easy to think about leaving everyone I knew behind.

The day of my departure finally arrived. My family drove me to the Los Angeles airport and I was surprised by a bunch of my friends upon our arrival, making it even harder than it already was for me to leave. Pictures were taken. Goodbyes and promises to keep in touch were said. Then once I got to the customs area, I looked back at my friends and family one last time. Not knowing when I'd see them again.

As I walked away, I could still hear their voices ... shouting their "goodbyes." But as I walked on, their voices gradually began to fade, one after the other.

After I was cleared by the customs personnel, I began my way to the departure gate. Soon enough, I felt this strong, sudden rush of emotion swell within my chest. There was a voice in my head saying, "What are you doing? You have no idea when you're gonna see them again." But I kept on walking towards the gate—fighting the temptation to look back—because I was still willing to follow my dream.

Then I got on the plane,
flew thousands of miles away,
and stepped foot in a new country.

And yes … I lived my dream …
plus more.

I ended up staying in the Philippines for four years, but in that short period, so much happened. Just to mention some of the highlights, it's because I got on that plane that I was able to:

- Witness many miracles
- Appear on television and radio
- Meet the "love of my life" and get married
- Give inspirational talks around the country
- See countless lives be set free from fear-based religion
- Enjoy deep friendships—unlike anything I've ever experienced before

Looking back, I guess I can say the risk was definitely worth it. It was a wild ride, to say the least. I'll admit, throughout the journey, there were many highs and many lows. And there were also many days where I'd be uncertain of what was gonna happen next. But you know what?—that's what made the whole experience so exciting.[1]

Keep in mind, moving to the Philippines was only one of my many dreams. I have a lot of dreams! In fact, many more of them were fulfilled once I moved back to America. And guess what, I'm *still* dreaming! Who says I have to stop, right? I'm on a roll, baby!

o o o

Like me, I believe you have dreams as well.

We all secretly do.

For some, their dreams are crystal clear—they know exactly what they wanna do, but they just haven't taken the first step yet. Then there are others, however, who have a general idea of what they wanna do, but the details are sort of blurry.

But the fact remains the same:
deep down,
beneath our selfish desires,
we all wanna make a positive mark …
in this world.

Whether our impact goes global or reaches only a few, we all want our lives to matter. We all wanna make a difference. And we all wanna believe we have a special gift to contribute to the rest of humanity.

But … "stuff happens."

We say things like,
"I'm not smart enough."
"I'm a nobody."
"I can't do it."
"I'm a failure."
"It's too late."
"I'm too old."
"I'm too young."
"Life's not about fun."
"I need to be more realistic."

Here's what I have to say concerning all those excuses:

They're are all a bunch of crap.

I'm serious. And if any of the above are the reasons keeping you from pursuing your dreams, then why did you even bother reading this book in the first place? So you can stare at a wall all day long and do nothing? No way!

You know there's something great about you!

Heck, *I know* there's something great about you!

So let's get down to it.

What's something you'd *absolutely love* to accomplish someday? In other words, what is *the* thing you'd wanna do that, if it were to happen, you'd be like, "Dude, that would be totally awesome!"

Don't think about the money or the abilities you need to do it—just think for a moment about the *possibility* of it happening. Are you feeling the excitement already?

Now before you get too excited, what would happen if you *didn't* do that *thing* you'd absolutely love to do? Have you thought about that too? Would you seriously wanna live the rest of your entire life wondering "what if"?

You see, it's about looking deep *within* yourself and figuring out what really makes *you* happy. So I'm not talking about doing what you think you "should" do or even what others expect of you. I'm talking about that *thing* which makes you feel alive!

Maybe you'd love to ...
write a book;
act in a movie;
become a teacher;
backpack in Europe;
open up a restaurant;
become a professional athlete;
become a professional dancer;
invent a new gadget;
build an orphanage;
be the president;
own a business;
or be an artist.

Now ask yourself this: *Why not?*

○ ○ ○

I know it sounds cheesy,
but what if your dream is your *destiny*?
What if it's something you were meant to do?

Mark Twain said:

> "The two most important days in your life are
> the day you are born and the day you find out why."

You can say, "But others have already written books, become singers, or started their own restaurant. Why would me doing what others have already done make any difference?"

Simple.

Those people aren't you!

You are you!

You have your own unique …
style,
flavor,
and twist.

Do yo' thang *your* way and add some variety to this world. Please, we need it. Imagine if everyone did everything exactly the same way.

BORING!

○ ○ ○

Think of the very *first anything*, for a moment.

The first car.
The first airplane.
The first telephone.
The first video camera.

Remember, these achievements first began as dreams in someone's mind. Were they impossible? To some people, yes. But to those who believed it was possible—no way! Their dreams were more real than the reality they were currently living in. They wanted it that bad.

And thankfully, the rest of us get to reap the benefits.

Helen Keller once said,

> "No pessimist ever discovered the secret of the stars,
> or sailed to an uncharted land, or opened a new
> doorway for the human spirit."

Think about going where no other person has gone before and/or doing what no other person has been able to do.

You can make history with your dream.

Don't follow the reasoning which says, "I'll see it when I believe it." Mind-blowing inventions never came from a self-limiting mentality like that. Rather, take the advice of Wayne Dyer who flips it and says, "I will see it when I believe it."

Did you get that? *When you believe … you will see.*

Folks, the only limitations are the ones between our ears. We create them with our minds—nowhere else.

Look at how technologically advanced we are these days—it's wild. Now think of how technology was fifty years ago. Twenty years ago. Five years ago. Or even just one year ago.

Technology never stops advancing!

Why? 'Cause people keep dreaming!

Isn't it crazy how we can video chat with someone on the other side of the world with a simple click of a button? Or what about the fact that we can fit thousands of songs in a pocket-size device? And doesn't it blow your mind that we now have everyday gadgets where we swipe the screen, just like in those futuristic movies that were shown decades ago?

The "future" is here.

And those who dared to bring the future into the present broke all boundaries placed on them, showing the rest of the world that *anything* is possible. Wait, let me qualify that last statement:

Anything is possible *to those who believe.*

Why?

As *The Alchemist* author Paul Coehlo puts it,

"Impossible is just an opinion."

So enough with the excuses already.

Procrastination gets you nowhere … fast.

Stop waiting for the "perfect" time.

Now is the time.

Not next year. Not next month. Not next week.

Not even tomorrow.

NOW.

Don't hand your life over to circumstances. Don't complain about your situation and be like, "It is what it is, and there's nothing I can do about it." That's just a bunch of bull, and you know it. Despite whatever situation you're in, you can and must still follow your dreams.

And if there seems to be no way, and you want something badly enough, then guess what?—you'll make a way! Period!

You don't have to *hope for* the future.
You don't even have to try and *predict* the future.

You can *create* the future.

So, for starters, begin acting great *today*. Today, be a great parent, a great spouse, a great friend, a great student—in big or small ways—and trust me, this greatness will flow into your future dream.

And since faith sees the end from the beginning,
your dream is already yours!

○ ○ ○

Can pursuing your dreams be scary at times? You betcha. But in order to make things happen, sometimes you gotta run after 'em hard without even looking back once—*believing that, somehow, things will work out for you in the end.*

Don't even think about quitting.

Learn the market.
Practice your skills.
Build your credibility.
Send out your resume.
Apply for the job you want.

Buy the equipment you need.

If your dream is to ...
appear on *American Idol*,
compete on *MasterChef*,
or strut your moves on *So You Think You Can Dance*,
there might be some risks you're gonna have to take.

What kinds of risks? Well, you might have to buy a plane ticket to a place you've never been to. Or you might have to quit your boring job. Or you might even have to skip a semester of college.

Whatever it is you have to do, remember ...
that as you work toward you dream ... be *patient*.
Some things don't happen overnight.

But trust me, the more steps you take, you're creating momentum, and momentum always builds toward something—even if you don't see it right away. Things will just "start happening" in unexpected ways.

Doors will swing open.
Opportunities will present themselves.
The right people will come your way.

And you'll begin to notice that what you want
starts wanting you.

○ ○ ○

Even though following your dreams can be exciting, I'm not saying at all that it's always gonna be easy. You might have to step out of your comfort zone here and there. You might even have days where you'll cry a lot tears, have long, sleepless nights, or even feel like giving up altogether.

But trust me, it'll all be worth it.

It may not look that way during those times,
but that's when you gotta "keep your eyes on the prize" the most.

Those tough moments, you gotta believe,
are somehow leading you closer to your destination.

So never give up.

I'll admit, there were countless times when I felt like giving up. But in those weak moments, I knew I had to keep on believing. I kept in mind that my challenges, no matter how discouraging they felt, weren't there to stay. And I reminded myself that I was gonna make it.

After going through the fire several times, I realized that what didn't kill me made me stronger. It was all part of the journey I was meant to live. And it was all part of the story I was meant to tell.

That being said, whenever you face challenges of any kind, or setbacks where things really aren't working out exactly the way you wanted them to—or people telling you you're never gonna make it—here's my advice:

never let those moments bring (or keep) you down.

Ever.

Protect your dreams.
Keep them safe.
Hold onto them.

And believe,
despite what you see,
you … *WILL* … make it.

It's your time to shine, friend.

The world is waiting for you.

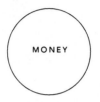

MONEY

LET IT BE LIKE A SHADOW

"Money is a great servant but a bad master."
Francis Bacon

"Anyone who lives within their means suffers from a lack of imagination."
Oscar Wilde

When my wife (Remy) first arrived in the Philippines, it only took three weeks before we finally met. There was an instant connection between us. And, without waiting for too long, we exchanged vows and celebrated this bond between us.

Now let me fill in some of the details.

Thankfully, during the wedding planning stages we found a place to hold the ceremony. To us, it couldn't have been more perfect.

So far, so good, right?
Well, there was a bit of a "problem."

Both of us didn't have "steady" jobs. And we only had enough money to make the down-payment for the reservation. But even though we weren't exactly "rolling in dough" at the time, we did have one thing.

Each other.

And that's all that mattered ... 'cause we were in love. We chose not to let the "lack" of money keep us from having the ceremony we wanted. But we also knew we had to step up our game, so to speak, and believe "for" bigger and better things for us.

Not wanting to let doubt and discouragement creep in—as a step of faith—we made the reservation for the ceremony location, not having any clue where the rest of the money we needed was gonna come from.

To continue exercising our faith, we decided to go on with the rest of the wedding planning—making a guest list and everything—and believing everything was gonna work out, somehow, for the best.

Let's fast-forward a couple months later. It was the week of our wedding—a Monday to be exact—and the ceremony was on Saturday, which was only a few days away.

Remy and I were hanging out at a mall and as we were going down an escalator, I turned to Remy and told her how much money we had in our bank account. Unfortunately, it still wasn't enough to cover the rest of the wedding expenses. But as we looked at each other with matching smiles on our faces, we both agreed that everything was *still* gonna work out.

Check this out ... on the *day before* our wedding ceremony (Friday) ... we received several thousand dollars! The amount was just what we needed! No, wait a minute, it was way more than what we needed!

The moment I received the money, I'll admit, my eyes started to "sweat" a bit. (Maybe the money was made of onions, I dunno.) But seriously though, I couldn't contain the gratitude I felt inside.

You see, deep down in my heart, I just knew the money was

gonna arrive on time. Actually, we both knew it, even if it meant it had to happen at the very last second, or in this case, last day. *How* were we gonna get it? Well, we just plain didn't know.

But it did anyway.

And that's what this chapter is about. It isn't necessarily about how to become a millionaire (although there's nothing wrong with wanting to become one). It's about having a healthy perspective about money and using the power within to create it—especially during the seemingly "impossible" situations.

○ ○ ○

Money.

When *you* think about it, how does it make you *feel*?

- *Worried* you don't have enough of it?
- *Excited* to get more of it?
- *Fear* you'll run out of it?

Here's the thing, whatever your *feelings* are about money, I guarantee they're a product of your thoughts. Trust me, I've felt all the emotions above, and one thing's for sure, these feelings all began in my mind.

Let me go through a couple of clichés about money I'm sure we've all heard before. I'll also include my short responses to each of them so you'll know why they don't make sense to me.

1. "*Money is the root of all evil.*"

   Well, if you think you're quoting the Bible, you're not. The Bible doesn't say money is the root of all evil. It actually says the "love of money" (greed) is the root of all evil. Stinkin' huge difference.

2. "*Rich people are corrupt.*"

   Not all of them. In fact, I know some people who became rich by working smart and hard. But you know what? I do know of some "poor"[1] people who've done some pretty shady things in order to get money. For instance, they've stolen and even killed for money. But I'm not gonna lump "them" altogether.

3. "*Being poor is spiritual.*"

   What's so spiritual about not being able to financially help others—and on top of that—not even being able to help yourself?

4. "*I'd rather be happy than have money.*"

   Why separate the two? Why can't you have both money *and* happiness?

5. *"I don't care about money."*

   Try telling that to the companies you pay your bills to. By the way, did you steal everything you own?

There are so many more clichés I could mention, but I'll throw these out for now just to get you thinking.

You see, money is neither good or bad.
(It's paper for goodness sake!)

What matters is … *how we make use of it.*

o o o

But two questions come to mind:

1. Why do some people seem to "attract" money more than others?

2. Why do others seem to constantly chase money away?

To help answer these questions, do you see a *connection* between your *beliefs* about money and your *situation* with money? Try putting two and two together. If your answer is "no," then let me keep explaining.

Do you *believe* the universe is …
for you?
Or against you?

Let's say, for example, you're facing a financial challenge. If you believe in a friendly and abundant universe, then isn't it possible for "random" and "unlikely" provisions to pop up in your life even during the seemingly "impossible" situations? Haven't you heard of those "rags-to-riches" stories where someone had nothing except a will to never give up—and with a little bit of "luck," ended up acquiring a lot of money in unexpected ways? Well, I have.

Also, try taking a look around you. If you've traveled a lot around the world, I think you'll understand what I'm about to say next.

You see, in my experience, I've literally seen both the rich and poor live side-by-side each other—so the environment doesn't matter. I've even seen people succeed and "fail" in the same business—so the type of job you want doesn't matter either. I've also seen people save money wisely and prosper, while others in fear hoard what they have and end up losing it all—so the amount of money one saves doesn't matter as well.[2]

What matters is …
thinking,
feeling,
and *acting* …
in a certain way …
that's in *alignment* with this friendly universe.

Then once you do,

everything else flows from there.

o o o

Maybe those struggling with money don't explicitly say things like "I hate money!" or "money is bad"—but the truth is, they can still have a poor view of money (no pun intended).

For instance, they constantly think and say things like:

"I can't afford that."
"I don't have enough."
"Money is hard to get."

Folks, these all stem from feelings of *lack*. Remember, if dominant thoughts and feelings (aka beliefs) create reality, should people be surprised if they get anything other than what they believe?

Think of it as a chain reaction.
Your thoughts …
affect your feelings,
and your feelings …
affect your actions.

So when you *think* there's not enough, or you *think* you can't afford something, or you *think* money is hard to get—then these *thoughts* will end up making you *feel* hopeless and fearful, won't they? And when you're *feeling* hopeless and fearful, you'll end up *acting* in a certain (wrong) way.

Sure, your conscious mind may want more money. But don't forget, your subconscious mind runs the show. And if your hidden beliefs are stuck in a "poverty" mentality, then it'll find expression in your life—whether you want it to or not.

Remember, everything is energy. If your mind is constantly thinking "debt, debt, debt" or "lack, lack, lack"—where will you be directing all your energy towards? What will you be creating?

Abundance?
(It doesn't take a rocket scientist to figure this one out.)

So instead of feeling lack all the time, start feeling good about money. No matter how crazy it sounds, start thinking, speaking, and acting like a "money magnet." Say things like "Money comes easy to me" or "I'm prosperous"—whatever will help you feel good.

'Cause once you raise your vibration,
your situation changes.

o o o

If money weren't an issue,
what would you do?

When I ask people this question, they get all excited and say things like "I wanna do this" and "I wanna do that." Then they go down a list of all the exciting things they wanna do and all the fun places they wanna visit. And let me just stress the point that it's always with huge smiles on their faces.

But does paper with images of dead presidents really make life more enjoyable? Why all the excitement?

I like the way Tim Ferriss, author of the bestseller *The 4-Hour Workweek* puts it,

> "People don't want to be millionaires—
> they want to experience what they believe
> only millions can buy."

That's it!

So it's not really about money after all.
It's the *experience* money can buy.

And life is all about experiences, right?

I believe it's in our nature to want better things in life. And I'm not only talking about living in a fancy mansion or driving expensive cars. Sometimes having a cozy, little home and a nice-looking car can give us the experience we're looking for. It really depends on the person.

But obviously, it still takes money to get these material things.

o o o

But what if a person only cares about money?

Now this is where a person's perception of money can be a problem. Those who acquire money only for themselves, screw others over to get more of it, and use it to do scandalous things, will definitely create more problems for themselves (and those around them).

See, you can have all the money in the world,
but here's the truth of the matter:

Life ain't that great when you only serve yourself.

I'm serious. Try making a god out of money and see how long your "happiness" will last. You'll eventually realize that money doesn't truly satisfy the deep longings of the human heart. You'll become a very shallow person—lose your sense of morale—and possibly feel the need to look over your shoulder every five minutes. And personally, I don't think that's a good way to live.

So don't let money (i.e., greed) control you.

o o o

But there's another mistake people make as well. For instance, someone says: "I don't need a lot of money. I only need enough to get by."

At first this can possibly sound admirable. But trust me, it's not.

Think about it. If you only have "enough," then there's not much to give away. And wouldn't you wanna be a giver?

For example, in order to give more, you obviously need more. So having more than enough money won't just benefit you, but others as well.

Having more than enough money can help you make financial contributions to ...
relief centers,
communities,
education,
businesses,
inventions,
and research—
helping to make this world a better place.

Not only that, your giving can help inspire others to wanna give as well!

Now let me take it a step further.

Giving is one thing,
but being a "cheerful giver" is even better.

It says a lot about you.

First, it says you're happy to help others.
Second, it says you have a "wealthy" mindset.
Third, it says you're not worried about supply.

Giving cheerfully also ends up not being a sacrifice at all.

In fact, you'll remember what a blessing it is to be a blessing—that's it's simply an overflow of what's going on inside you.

In other words, when you give from the heart,
you don't "have to" give,
you "get to" give.

Cheerful giving doesn't always have to be huge chunks of money either. As Mother Teresa said, "It's not how much we give but how much love we put into giving." It's the heart and motive which ultimately matters.

And don't forget, wanting to get rid of poverty in this world isn't only done through giving, it's also done through *inspiring*. Sure, relieving a person's suffering for a moment is great, but inspiration can last for several lifetimes. So let your giving motivate others to get out of the rut they're in and help them actually wanna do something about their situation.

o o o

Someone can say, "Josh, you don't understand. What happened to me financially wasn't my fault. I had no control over it."

Look,
if you're in a financially tough situation now,
it is your fault if you continue to stay in it.

As always, it comes down to *choice*.

I'll never forget the story told by Rhonda Byrne in her book *The Power*. She mentions the time when, at one point, she "reached an all-time low with money" in her life.

Let me do a break-down of what happened:

Several of her credit cards were charged up.
Her apartment was mortgaged to the limit.
Her company was in debt for millions of dollars.
She had no idea how to pay off her staff's wages.

So she, in her own words, "took a drastic action."

On a Friday,
she withdrew several hundred dollars from her credit card account. (Which, of course, she could've used to pay bills and buy food with.) Then she started handing out $50 bills to random people on the street. (She said, for the first time in her life, she *felt love* for money.)

Then on Monday,
something "astounding happened."
$25,000 ended up in her bank account![3]

How the heck did that happen?!

Like Rhonda, we all have the potential to face financial challenges from time to time. But the solution, as she demonstrated, wasn't in the feeling of fear. Instead, no matter how weird it sounds, the solution was in ... are you ready?

Feeling good.

Yup, that's right. *Feeling good* (or in Rhonda's case, feeling love) puts you at a higher vibration than when you're feeling sad. And being at a higher vibration, well, somehow "attracts" more positivity into your life. Don't ask me how it all works because I don't know. All I do know is that it does work. This is why it's so important to stay positive during the seemingly difficult times.

○ ○ ○

Ever hear the story mentioned in Florence Shinn's writings about a priest who visited a nunnery in France?[4]

According to the story, a nun in despair told a priest they only had one piece of silver left and that all the sisters were afraid the children were gonna go hungry.

Then the priest told the nun to give him the coin.
So she gave him the coin.

And what did the wise priest do with it? Buy food?
Nope. *He threw the coin out the window!*

The priest told the nun to "rely entirely upon God."[5]

Within a short time, friends came with lots of food and gifts of money.

Now,
I didn't share this story so you could throw away all your money.

My point is this: *trust* in a friendly universe.

If you ever find yourself in a situation where you have absolutely no clue what to do next—instead of stressing out—try relaxing for a moment while waiting for the next step. And believe that good things are coming your way.

Just so you know, there are countless stories of millionaires who have lost a lot of money—didn't let it phase them—and somehow "miraculously" gained the money all back again.

How?

As I've heard several of them say,
"If I lost a million. No problem.
I can *create* it again."

○ ○ ○

One interesting encounter I had was when I met a group of strangers. They contacted me over the phone one day and I had absolutely no idea who they were. They were familiar with my work and wanted to meet me in person—even willing to hop on a plane to make it happen. I felt confused, yet honored by their gesture. So I decided to meet with them at a restaurant near my home. We talked for several hours getting to know each other, sharing amazing stories of how money came to us in sometimes unexplainable ways.

I'll never forget what one of them said to me: "Josh, people use the money they have and decide what they want. *We decide what we want and the money comes."*

Here's the thing, if you really want something badly, you either have the money for it, or you don't. If you do have the money, then good. But if you don't have the money, well then, there's one thing you gotta do.

Create it.

Don't be concerned with how much is in your bank account. I know this can sound crazy. But remember, it's the "crazy" people who are able to think outside the box and believe "impossible" things.

Here's how to go about the creation process:

1. It starts with *desire*. What is it you want?

2. Believe that what you want is *already* yours. (Your emotions will make evident your dominant thoughts.)

3. "Act as if" you're receiving it. I'm not kidding. Let your thoughts, words, feelings, and actions be consistent with

one another, demonstrating that what you want is already yours. Do this for however long it takes.

And no matter what, always prepare for success, not failure.

Don't think small either. As you take baby steps in the beginning, take bigger steps of faith as you go along. Challenge yourself. It's the only way to expand your "wealth consciousness."

'Cause when you think bigger, you'll obviously see bigger results.

o o o

I know, I know. If you're skeptical, you can say you did make a list of all the things you wanted, had the faith for it, and some (if not all) of your desires just didn't manifest.

OK, but here's the million dollar question:

What was the *level of belief* you had for the things which didn't manifest? Think about it, on a scale from 1-10 (10 meaning you had absolutely no doubt), how high was your expectation?

Trust me, it's one thing for you to *desire* "big" things, but it's another thing for you to *believe* you can actually have them. Don't be surprised if you don't get the things you outwardly confess to believe yet you inwardly doubted all the while. Or to put it another way, don't ask for "big" things if you still have a hard time believing "for" even the "little" things.[6]

But then again, where your level of expectation is high, focus on those things specifically. Trust me, it's just matter of time, baby.

o o o

It's always good to be thankful for what you have right now. Start counting your blessings one by one—even if it's just you having a few coins in your pocket, the simple clothes on your back, and comfortable shoes to walk in. There's no need to wait for more money to arrive to feel prosperous. You can feel prosperous now.

You might be thinking,
"But *how* do I get more blessings to come my way?"

Don't worry about it.

I'm serious. I'm not saying you shouldn't think of different ways to make money work for you. But what I am saying is that you shouldn't *worry* about it. There's a difference. Your goal is to trust, to feel good, and to follow any hunches you have.

You know that "inner voice" we all sometimes tend to ignore? Yup, that one. Follow it for once. You won't regret it.

In Florence Shinn's book *The Game of Life and How to Play It*, she mentions a story about a discouraged woman who only had "eight dollars and a hunch." One time, a woman went to see Florence for some prosperity treatment. Florence spoke prosperity into her life and asked the woman to follow her own intuition. The woman said she had a hunch to go home. Thankfully, she had just enough cash for carfare. Once she got home, in a "miraculous" way, she received thousands of dollars through a friend.

The takeaway: *never violate a hunch.*

It can literally multiply whatever you have in an instant.

○ ○ ○

Here are some concluding tips you can try:

1. Make vision boards of things you want, places you wanna visit, and experiences you wanna have. Put it in a place where you'll always see it—like in your bedroom, or near your study desk. But don't just look at the vision boards—"feel the feeling" of already receiving the things you're looking at.

2. Distance yourself from people who bring you down or instill doubt. Instead, hang out with like-minded folks who can inspire you to reach your financial goals. I once watched comedian Steve Harvey tell Oprah in an interview, "If nine of your friends are broke. You're going to be the tenth one. ... Stop telling your dreams to small-minded people."

3. Grab bills of money and lay them out in front of you.

Then hold a stash in your hands and "feel the wealth." Close your eyes and imagine the bills multiplying. Smell it. Feel a positive connection to it. Be friends with it. Sounds weird, I know. But the purpose is to do whatever it takes [for you] to feel good about money.

4. Pay it forward. Pay for a person's meal or a stranger's coffee behind you at a drive-thru. Leave bigger tips than usual at restaurants. Who knows, it might "make someone's day." It's good to give, remember?

5. Learn to "pay yourself first" and set up an automatic investment account. Instead of letting the money in your savings account just sit there and do nothing, try investing your money in stocks and let it grow.[7]

6. Learn different ways to make passive income. It's easy to make money online these days in more than one stream. Did you know you can earn money by writing blogs, making videos, and recording podcasts?

7. Whenever you receive a bill (the ones you owe), close your eyes and say, "Thank you that this bill is already paid." *Feel the gratitude*. And don't let your spending revolve all around that bill either. Expect more money to flow into your life and live according to your expectation (faith).

8. Keep affirming yourself by saying "I'm getting richer and richer everyday." Sing it in the shower. Say it while you're waiting in line. Mumble it while you're falling asleep.

Whatever you do.

Think abundance.
Speak abundance.
Feel abundance.

Then,
as you *act* accordingly,
trust the universe to do its thang.

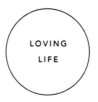

LOVING
LIFE

THE ART OF WONDER

"Some people feel the rain, others just get wet."
Bob Marley

"We should concern ourselves,
not so much with the pursuit of happiness,
but with the happiness of pursuit."
from *Hector and the Search for Happiness*

A few days ago I was at a lodge with some friends and we decided to watch Jim Carrey's hilarious film *Yes Man*.

In the beginning of the movie, Carrey plays a character named Carl who says "no" to basically every opportunity presented to him. And this pattern isn't without its consequences. Sadly, Carl ends up living a mundane and boring life because of it.

Luckily, at what seems to be the perfect time, Carl runs into his old friend Nick. Nick boasts to Carl about his life magically changing for the better because of one simple word.

"Yes."

Nick encourages Carl to attend the seminar where he learned this so-called "secret" to an exciting life and lets him know that he too can become what is called a "Yes! Man." Carl, frustrated with life—realizing he's swiftly heading nowhere, ends up going to the seminar.

During the seminar, Carl notices the audience repeatedly shouting *yes!* every time a question is asked by Terrence, who is the main speaker of the event. Unexpectedly, Terrence puts Carl on the spot, rushes towards him with a microphone, and let's everyone in on their conversation:

Terrence: You're dead, Carl. You say no to life. And therefore you're not living. You make up excuses to the people around you and to yourself.

Carl: Wow. *(Overwhelmed)*

Terrence: We're gonna make a covenant, Carl.
Do you want to make a covenant?

Carl: Umm ...

Terrence: The word is "yes," Carl.

Carl: Yes ... Yes.

Terrence: Once you leave this building ... every time an opportunity presents itself ... no matter what it is ... you will say "yes."

Carl: Yes! YES!

This encounter with Terrence changed Carl's life forever.

From that point on, Carl says "yes" to absolutely everything presented to him—no matter how "crazy" the request is. He goes from one wild adventure to another, doing things he probably wouldn't have done if he hadn't made the covenant with Terrence in the first place.

Carl ...
goes bungee jumping;
learns to play the guitar;
learns to speak Korean;
gets into a fight;

gives money away;
and luckily, meets the love of his life.

The world, because of this one word, became his playground.

After watching the film, I stepped outside the lodge and lingered on the dock near the lake. Before me was an amazing view: the water was serene … a variety of trees surrounded me … and as I looked up into the sky, the sun was about to set.

I was reminded of how the world was my playground too—
ready for me to …
explore,
discover,
and even create.

Then I started shouting, *Yes! Yes! Yes!* (I'm kidding)

As I've heard it said before, life's meant to be *enjoyed*, not *endured*. There's too much good in the world for us to say "yes" to. And there's not enough "bad" in this life to keep us from enjoying ourselves.

You see,
life doesn't begin or end with any particular location or activity.

Life happens wherever you are,
with whatever activity you're doing,
and whoever you're with … in *this* moment.

I understand that, like Carl in *Yes Man*, life can get a bit dull sometimes—doing the same ol' routine every single day. It can reach a point where there's nothing left to look forward to anymore. You get up, go to work, then go home and sleep. Crazy thing is, some of us do this for decades without experiencing much excitement in between (or during) those activities. The only thing that would break the cycle is to *really* go to sleep—"six-feet under," that is—if you know what I mean.

What about you?

What gets you out of bed every day? Work? School? Taking care of the kids? Or do you, like a lot of people, not have any stinkin' clue why you do what you do?

Whatever your reasons are for getting out bed, I'm not saying you need to go skydiving, or anything like that, to live life to the fullest.

But is life still interesting and exciting for you?
Do you still experience *wonder*?

If you're already loving your life, then good. I'm happy for you. But if you have entered the world of "boring land" and catch yourself yawning every five minutes, I guarantee it isn't because you have *actually* entered such a place. Truth is, it's your *mind* which perceives your world to be so.

And I bet you didn't always feel this way.

I'm sure most of us can remember how as children, we were constantly filled with awe. Our world, I guess you can say, was pretty darn good. For instance, every little object given to us became a toy. Every place we visited became an unfolding adventure. And every time somebody surprised us with a little "peek-a-boo," it led to a belly quaking with laughter.

Do *you* remember?

Whether we …
saw the colors of a rainbow,
heard the sounds of music,
everyone and everything …
widened our eyes and brought about a sense of wonder.

Nothing was ..
trivial,
dull,
or too simple.

But then … we grew up.

The exciting became the routine.
The extraordinary became the mundane.
And our imaginations learned to settle for "reality."

But. (Let's not lose hope just yet.)

Imagine doing things you've never done,
going to places you've never been to,

and seeing things you've never seen before.

Imagine *creating your day.*

Remember, if you don't love the life you're living right now and keep doing the same things you've always done, then don't be surprised if the same results exhaust you in the coming years.

The question is, *How can you learn to love life even more?*

The rest of this chapter will reveal several perspectives and practices I've learned which have helped me to relax, enjoy and love life even more.

I hope they can be of some use to you.

OK, let's go!

o o o

I wanna begin with a cool (yet insightful) exercise:[1]

1. Take about a minute to look around wherever you are and count the number of things you see that are *red.*

2. Now, without taking your eyes off this page, try thinking of everything around you that's *yellow.*

(Please don't blame me for giving bad instructions.)

Here's my point: There's probably a bunch of yellow around you, but the thing is, you didn't *notice* it. Why?

Because you were *only looking for red.*

See, I believe the same goes with life as well.

Your quality of life …
your happiness …
your joy …
depends on what you notice …
every …
single …
day.

It's a state of mind.

Realize that no matter how you're feeling right now (even if you feel good), you can always feel better!

For starters, one way to feel better than what you're feeling now is by showing something all of us are capable of doing, no matter how challenging life can get at times.

And it's this: *Gratitude.*

There's a really cool experiment on Youtube called *The Science of Happiness.*[2] What it reveals about the power of gratitude is eye-opening.

Here's what happened during the experiment:

First, volunteers were given a test revealing their level of happiness at the moment.

Second, they were asked to close their eyes and think of an important person in their lives.

Third, they were told to write down as much as they could of why this person was so important to them.

But the experiment wasn't over just yet. On the spot, they were asked to pick up a phone and call the person they wrote about—even if the person was out of the country. Then once the person picks up, they're supposed to read everything they wrote down on the paper to them.

And so … one by one … they did.

What happened during these phone calls?
Shyness.
Tears.
Smiles.
Laughter.

But before the volunteers left, they were given another test to reveal their level of happiness *after* the experiment. It's interesting because, according to the results, happiness increased between four and nineteen percent.

What's even more interesting is the fact that the volunteer who experienced the *biggest boost in happiness* was, get this, the *least happiest person* at the beginning of the experiment!

You see, no matter how crappy you're feeling right now, gratitude can change things.

o o o

As I mentioned in an earlier chapter, I struggled a lot with my underdeveloped right hand. I remember those countless times as a child when I'd be sitting in the backseat of my parents' car looking at my hand, and start crying silently. Yup, my "sadness level"—concerning this issue—was really that bad!

For many years, I focused so much on how "different" I was from those around me. This sort of tunnel vision kept me so focused on what I didn't have and the things I *thought* I couldn't do—which only reinforced that horrible feeling that life was indeed unfair.

But you know how my perception of life got better? It was through a simple *shift in focus.* I chose to start noticing something else.

I stopped focusing on the *why.*
And I started focusing on the *what.*

What can I be thankful for now? I'd ask myself.

I started being thankful for the fact that, although my right hand is not fully developed, I still have a palm and little fingers to work with. Why is this so important for me?

- Well, in elementary school, it actually helped me balance my body when I started getting into breakdancing.

- I can dribble a basketball with it.

- I can play video games with it. (I'm pretty good too!)

- I can balance stuff on it—things like plates and other objects I need to carry around.

- I can even type this book on my laptop!

In other words, looking for the so-called "littlest" benefits of having what I have improved my love for life significantly. (When you *look* for something, you'll *see* it, remember?)

Now, I know of some people who don't even have palms, hands, or even any arms. But I'm not here to compare myself with others and see who has it better or worse. We all have our own challenges to deal with. You have your own and, well, this one was mine.

The question is, *Will you start focusing on what you have?*

It takes a lot of courage to have an "attitude of gratitude" during the "dark" times. But once you have it, it empowers you. It helps you realize it's not the end of the world (contrary to what many religious folks say). And it enables you to see and feel the light, no matter how dark you *perceive* the world to be at any particular moment.

But most of all, gratitude helps you to *see* that …
life …
is …
good.

You don't need to wait till you get thinner.
You don't need to wait till you get your dream job.
You don't need to wait till you meet the "perfect" mate.

Happiness is NOW.

And once you start seeing life this way,
it starts looking so much better.

o o o

"But Josh, "you might say, "you don't understand. I'm thankful for a lot of things. But I still have a job to keep, kids to raise, and bills to pay."

Ah yes, I think I smell that old stench of *worrying* going on. It's weird, but some people feel like they have to worry—as though it's the "responsible" thing to do. For instance, when things are looking too good to be true, they *find* something to worry about—always adding the word "but" after saying something positive.

Let me just say this, if you're the type of person who constantly worries and adds the word "but" after every good thing, well, you can kick all those "buts" right in the arse! (Wait a minute. That came out wrong. But I think you get my point.)

Worry is rooted in *fear.*

And sorry to burst anyone's bubble, but worrying *isn't* the responsible thing to do. It's an unnecessary "obligation" to have. And it's simply a waste of time and energy.

Whenever your thoughts are scattered everywhere—either dwelling on the past or anxious about the future—here's what you can do:

Be still.
Be present.[3]

Learn to get "out of your mind," so to speak.

You may not be *aware* of it, but you do have something which can remove all worry (and other fear-based emotions) in an instant.

Awareness.

Funny thing is, many of us aren't even aware of awareness.

That being said,
I want you to try a couple of things right now. Ready?

OK, relax and *pay attention* to your breathing for a moment.

Now, what do you *hear* around you?
(Close your eyes if it helps)

Dogs barking?
Music playing?
Cars passing by?
Crickets chirping?
Children laughing?

Now, what do you *feel* in and on your body?
(Close your eyes if it helps)

Heat?
Energy?
A cool breeze?
Tingly sensations?

Next, what do you *see* in front of you?
(Don't judge, just observe.)

Clouds in the sky?
Designs on a wall?
An insect on the floor?
The color of your friend's eyes?

Did you notice anything else?

Once you became aware of *any* of these things …
all your worries …
all your stress …
all your fears …
simply *disappeared.*

That's the power of awareness, folks.

You don't need to bungee jump off a bridge or run across hot coals to be fully engaged in the moment. There are less adrenaline-rushing activities you could do everyday to stop your thoughts from jumping all over the place.

Once again, it's all a matter of what you're noticing—
what you're paying attention to.

When you hear a beautiful symphony playing in the background as you stroll through a park, will you stop and listen?

When the person you've committed your life to is standing right in front of you, will you stop and look into their eyes?

When you take a walk through the neighborhood on a hot summer day, will you stop and notice the sunset in a distance?

You see, no matter what negative story you're creating in your mind right now (i.e., worry), life is still happening all around you.

Will you …
see it,
touch it,
taste it,
smell it,
hear it,
as if for the very first time?

'Cause you can experience it all … right … *now*.

○ ○ ○

One thing I love about my wife is that she hasn't lost her child-like wonder. Recently, we arrived home late one night and, as I went to check our mailbox, I heard her voice behind me yelling, "Hey Josh, a snail!" I turned around and started laughing. Once I saw the tiny creature, I couldn't help but be reminded of all the times as a kid when I'd put salt on them—or the times where I'd burn ants with a magnifying glass. (OK, maybe these aren't the best memories to share for insect lovers.)

My point is that, in those moments, not an inch of worry was in me. (Sorry, next time I'll think of more positive insect stories to share.) I was simply a little boy filled with excitement and curiosity—amazed by the little creatures moving around on the ground. It was just me and my bugs. (But after I burned them, I guess it was just me. That was bad. OK, I'll stop.)

Whether it's a snail you're looking at … or clouds forming

shapes in the sky ... always remember to:

Watch.
Observe.
Pay attention.

And allow the wonder to take over. Trust me, it will.

o o o

Gratitude ... happiness ... wonder ... these are all great.

But what is your *purpose*?

You see, when people use the word "purpose," they're usually referring to a career, a goal, or to something in the future.

But there's another way to understand "purpose"—one which is essential to fulfilling what you want to do in life. I learned this insight from good ol' Eckhart Tolle's book *A New Earth*.

There are two kinds of purpose:

1. *Inner* purpose (primary)
2. *Outer* purpose (secondary)

Your inner purpose is to awaken.
Your outer purpose changes and varies from person to person.

Let me keep explaining.

Let's say, for example, you feel that your purpose and meaning in life is to be a great teacher. Nothing wrong with that. In fact, wanting to educate people is admirable. But here's a question, *What happens when you're no longer teaching?*

Or what if, as Eckhart mentions, you feel your purpose and meaning in life is to care for your kids? This is an admirable thing to do as well, *but what happens when they grow up and no longer depend on you?*

It's interesting because in both these instances,
your purpose and meaning in life rely on others being …
less smarter, and less responsible than you.

Not only that, but these kinds of purposes are unstable and can change. I mean, think of any vocation you want to pursue. What if your purpose is to be a good doctor, or a police officer, or a firefighter—or whatever—once again, the *stability* of these becoming your life's purpose and meaning is still the same: there isn't any.

For instance, I doubt you heal the sick, fight crime, or put out fires 24/7.[4] But if these things are what gives your life purpose and meaning, what happens in between these *activities*? Is your life no longer meaningful during certain hours of the day? Does your purpose suddenly disappear when you're no longer doing what these jobs require? Of course not.

That's why these are all considered to be *secondary/outer* purposes.

And that's why there must be a deeper kind of purpose—the kind which "flows into what you do"—which brings us back to the importance of your primary/inner purpose (to *awaken*).

Think of it this way. Right now, you're reading this book. As you turn the page, your primary purpose isn't to seek and gain understanding. That's your secondary purpose. Your primary purpose is to do what?

Turn the page.

Or, as a parent, when you're changing your baby's diaper, your primary purpose isn't to provide and care for your baby (although it's a worthy cause). Once again, that's your secondary purpose. Your primary purpose is to do what?

Change your baby's diaper.

Or let's say you wanna give a sweet, little kiss to your spouse in the bedroom—so you start walking towards him or her. Your primary purpose is walking to the bedroom. Your secondary purpose is to kiss your spouse. But the moment you start kissing your spouse, guess what?—*that* becomes your primary purpose.

It's all about experiencing what Eckhart calls "the power of now." It's about being fully engaged in the present moment—experiencing the sights and sounds, tastes and touch, smells—the whole shebang.

Each moment, believe or not, is all we really have. Think about it. The previous moment is gone. The future moment isn't even here yet. (From a linear perspective, that is.) But we all have something very special right now to experience.

This moment.
Don't miss it.

○ ○ ○

Here are some tips you can try as we conclude this chapter:

1. Say "thank you" for everything you become aware of. Air to breathe. Ears to take in all the sounds around you. Legs to walk with. Food to eat. Water to drink. A home to belong to. A bed to sleep in. A car to drive. Friends. Family. The rain. The sun. The sky. Trees. Flowers. Someone opening a door for you. Someone giving you a smile or even another chance. Anything … I mean anything can help brighten up your day. It's all a matter of noticing, remember?

2. Talk with strangers and do random acts of kindness. It's good to connect with other fellow human beings once in a while. It's also a good reminder you're not alone. Who knows? A person you meet might end up being a good friend, or even something more (wink, wink).

3. (As always) Laugh and laugh and laugh and laugh. It's good for you both physically and emotionally. It keeps

you looking and feeling young. It can even help you through difficult times. 'Cause once you stop taking life so seriously, the "big" problems no longer seem so big anymore.

4. Take risks. I read the following line from somewhere: "Do one thing every day that scares you." Who knows, one decision can change your life forever. And it only takes a second or two to actually make that decision.

5. Go on a mini or even a grand vacation. It doesn't even have to be far. Just drive somewhere you've never been to. Take a break from routine.

6. Find a new hobby. Learn a sport. Take up dancing. Learn to cook. Who knows, you might end up being an expert at something.

o o o

Life is a gift.
Today is a gift.

Today isn't just another day.

Some say we should live each day as though it were our *first*. Others say we should live each day as though it were our *last*.

I say, no matter which approach you take to life:

Live it well.

And soak it all in.

...REVEALED

"New beginnings are often disguised as painful endings."

Lao Tzu

"There are far, far better things ahead
than any we leave behind."

C.S. Lewis

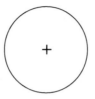

The year was 2006.

I was standing outside the university library, getting ready to speak at an event. It felt like just another day. All I was planning on doing was sharing how I came to the belief that *all things—including miracles—are possible to those who believe*. In fact, I spoke on the very same topic just one week prior at a conference in Los Angeles.

But before I started walking toward the auditorium, I thought, *I'll just do what I always do. I'll keep my right hand in my pocket the entire time just like at the conference I did last week. No big deal. I don't wanna deal with one of my biggest fears today while I'm up there.*

So, without a worry in the world—
excited to inspire others with a positive message—
off I went to my speaking engagement.

Shortly after I entered the building, I kid you not, something out of the ordinary happened to me.

I heard a very *distinct* voice.

But it wasn't just any voice. This voice was *gentle*, yet *firm*. It didn't sound or feel like the usual voice in my head—especially because of what I heard it say. It was like an *internal audible voice* ... interrupting my thoughts.

Call it "God," "The Universe," "My Higher self"—

call it whatever you want.

All I know is that the voice was crystal clear. And it said:

"You are going to show your hand today."

That's it. That's all I heard.

I immediately froze in my tracks.

While my eyes were wandering from left to right, my mind was wondering what in the world had just happened.

So what did I do next? I began panicking ... *big time!*

I started pacing back and forth in the back of the auditorium—freaking out—not sure if I was ready to do what I'd heard the voice say.

Was it a command? A prediction?

Whatever it was, one thing's for sure, I absolutely didn't wanna do it!

Once I was called up to the front, I seriously didn't know what to do anymore. As I began talking, and with my right hand still in my pocket, I felt extremely uncomfortable. My voice trailed off and the words left me. Those listening were probably wondering what it was that I was hesitating to do or say.

Why the hell am I doing this? I was thinking. *Why now? I mean, I've gotten so used to not doing it for so long, is there really any point in giving it another try?*

"Ugh, this is really hard. I'm sorry." I said.

It got quiet.

Without warning, a voice from somewhere in the audience yelled out, "We love you, Josh!"

"Whatever!" I jokingly responded.

The crowd broke out in laughter.
(Humor is always a great defense mechanism, by the way.)

There was a long pause.

"There was something here," I continued, "that I wasn't gonna share 'cause it was too personal … (long pause) … anyways … (long pause) … sorry."

And then I burst into tears.

There I was … standing there … vulnerable … with all eyes on me. I tried to remove my right hand from my pocket several times, but I just couldn't. And as my mind began to be overwhelmed with painful childhood memories, the fear deepened even more.

I started doubting myself. I wasn't sure whether or not I could go through with it anymore. It was like a tennis match of *"you can do it"* and *"you can't do it"* playing live in my head. And the second voice looked like it was winning.

Then, a close friend stood up from his seat, moved to the center of the aisle, and looked directly at me. He gave me this intense look with his eyes and slightly nodded his head. (Yup, it was the same look and nod Mr. Miyagi gave Daniel-san right before his special kick in the film *The Karate Kid*!)

With tears running down my face, and with a shaking voice, I said, "So if you [audience] could do me a favor and just ... do your best to respond in a way where it just won't hurt me."

Suddenly, at what seemed to come out of nowhere, a courage from deep within made an unexpected appearance.

And then ...
while my eyes were fixed to the ground ...
terrified to even peek at the audience's different reactions ...
it happened.

I took my right hand out of my pocket ...
and for the first time in my life ...
I held it up high for everyone to see.

Then ... with my hand still up in the air ... I found the courage to finally look at the crowd. And what I saw was something I'll never, ever forget.

I saw people's eyes … staring,
but to my surprise …
they *weren't* looking at my hand.

Instead, I saw them looking …
straight into my *eyes* …
and ultimately …
into my *heart*.

I couldn't believe what I was seeing.

At that exact moment … something in me changed. A surge of confidence arose from within, and I began speaking with such an intense conviction—to the point where many students in the audience were moved to tears as well.

Then, as my talk drew to a close, another unexpected thing happened. A girl who was crying in the audience spoke up and asked me to help her. So I invited her to come to the front where I was to find out what was wrong. Once she stood next to me, she told us all about an insecurity she had with her own body. But she didn't stop there. She even found the courage to *show* us the part of her body she was struggling with.

Being moved with compassion by what I just saw, I asked people from the audience to come forward so they could speak into her life. Without any hesitation, several people did. And after a couple of minutes, I looked around the room and saw groups of students encouraging one another.

As more and more tears began to run down the faces of all these different people—of some who didn't even really know each other until bare moments ago—their loud cries started to be heard all throughout the auditorium.

These were ...
tears of joy ...
tears of pain ...
and tears of healing.

This went on all the way past midnight.

And every single second of it was impossible to forget.

o o o

You see, there can come a time in life when that one decision you make can change your reality forever.

That painful day back in 2006 ... where I experienced truly unexpected, unconditional love ... the overcoming of fear ... and a sudden leap of faith ... created for me ... a *new beginning.*

Since then,
that one night has helped me to ...
become more open about my struggles,
and believe I can accomplish anything ...
no matter how scary things may appear to be.

I finally realized that *love* has been there all along ... all throughout my life ... from the day I was born ... to even this very moment. Yet it wasn't until that day at the auditorium that I was *awakened* to this ever-present reality to such a degree that it catapulted me beyond all of my self-set boundaries.

That's what love *does*.

And *that's* what love can do for *you*.

Like my story,
you have absolutely nothing to fear.

You're *safe* in love.

Love was, is, and always will be ...
the answer to the deepest, unspoken questions in life.

But then again, you *already* know this.

You've *always* known this.

So let this book just be a simple *reminder*:

LOVE YOURSELF.

'Cause what this world needs is ...
a *greater*,
a more *fearless*,
and a more *loving* ...
YOU.

NOTES

INTRO: *What Do You See?*

1. This is a phrase my friend and bestselling author, Greg Kuhn, loves to say.

SUBCONSCIOUS: *"I Have Two What?!"*

1. This example of my wife learning how to drive came to mind when I first heard Dr. Bruce Lipton mention the "driving analogy" in an interview he did for a podcast. It's such a great way to explain the power of the subconscious mind.

CREATING: *Bending Reality 101*

1. For the sake of brevity, the conversation between Neo and Morpheus is condensed from its original length.
2. A big shout-out to my friend, Greg Kuhn, for chatting on the phone with me that one day. Thanks for helping me break down all this "science stuff" into simpler language.
3. I got this quote from the book *What the Bleep Do we Know!?* It's an awesome book which brings together both science and religion to help explain the universe. Not only that, it's also a movie. Go watch it.
4. For many years I studied books on positive confession—particularly the ones on healing. But the whole idea of fueling our "prayers" (words) with feeling was never truly brought to my attention until I first discovered the works of Gregg Braden. I first heard (or noticed) the phrase "feeling the feeling" while watching one of his lectures on Youtube. This insight has definitely revolutionized (and simplified) my understanding of positive speaking.
5. One of the most influential thought leaders, Neville Goddard, wrote an entire book called *Feeling is the Secret*, showing how feelings help shape one's reality. It's a book I highly recommend.
6. For the sake of brevity, this is a condensed version of the story found in Gregg Braden's book.

7. As Gregg mentions in the book, he can't say with 100% certainty that David's prayer played any role in the storms that followed their time together. But he also admits, which is important to point out is that—within a matter of hours—the weather in northern New Mexico *did* change that day.
8. These examples are found in Travis Taylor's book *The Science Behind the Secret*.
9. Greg Kuhn is the bestselling author of the *Why Quantum Physicists* ... series.

3: LOVING YOURSELF: *Everything Else Flows From There*

1. You can read more about this in an article entitled *Jumpers* which appeared in *The New Yorker* magazine in 2003. Here's the link: http://www.newyorker.com/magazine/2003/10/13/jumpers.
2. There's a documentary about the suicides called *The Bridge* (2006). The director, Eric Steel, interviewed the friends and relatives of the suicide victims.

4. HEALING: *Living Naturally "Supernatural"*

1. Throughout the book you'll notice me putting quotations around the word "disease" (or names of diseases). Obviously, labels are simply given to describe something. But I sometimes think labels can do more harm than good as you'll soon read later on in the chapter.
2. Of course babies are the exception. Another factor as well can be the environment.
3. To date, Lissa's book is one of my favorite books on healing. It's extremely informative and it summarizes a lot of what I've learned about the subject throughout the years.
4. Everything I write about epigenetics here is what I've learned from *The Biology of Belief* and the various podcasts I've heard Dr. Bruce Lipton interviewed on. So I'm basically just paraphrasing here. If you're interested in this subject, get his eye-opening book!
5. You can read more about the power of perception in Bruce Lipton's book *The Honeymoon Effect*. Don't be fooled by the title. Although it's primarily a book about creating loving relationships, he incorporates quantum physics, biochemistry, and psychology to explain the science behind the

magic of love.

6. You can read more interesting stories and control group studies in Joe Dispenza's book *You Are the Placebo*. He also shares an inspiring story of how he healed his own body after a serious injury he suffered from.
7. I heard Wayne Dyer share this unfortunate (yet insightful) story on a Youtube video called *Dr. Wayne Dyer & Dr. Bruce Lipton, Pt.1*. You can watch it here: https://www.youtube.com/watch?v=ylmwoJDYGjk.
8. Remember, I'm not too fond of using labels for diseases. Like Anita Moorjani's 's yoga master, I believe they're just words—sometimes causing unnecessary fear. But for the purpose of this book, I'm only using labels to communicate.
9. I'm reminded of a story in Jose Silva's book, *The Silva Method*, of a woman who wore glasses for twenty-seven years because of nearsighted astigmatism. She repeatedly told herself, "Every time I blink my eyes, they will focus accurately, like the lens of a camera." In two weeks she no longer needed to wear glasses except for when she had to read.

5. DREAMS: *Jump. Fall. Fly.*

1. I go into more detail in my first book *So You Thought You Knew*, if you wanna read more about it.

6. MONEY: *Let It Be Like A Shadow*

1. Wealth and poverty are *ultimately* a mindset.
2. I learned much of these ideas concerning money from reading two classic works on the subject. One is Napoleon Hill's *Think and Grow Rich* and the other is Wallace Wattles' *The Science of Getting Rich*. Get 'em. They're classics for a reason.
3. The money came from shares she bought from her friend's company. It was totally unexpected because the value of the shares never increased. Then suddenly, they did. Her huge step of faith showed how much trust she had in a friendly universe.
4. This story is found in *The Complete Works of Florence Scovel Shinn*. I highly recommend reading all of her books. The stories she shares are definitely faith-builders.

5. I understand some of my readers may not believe in God. It's all good. But I'm assuming we all believe in a universe, right? Question is, *Is this universe friendly?*
6. Another issue to think about is the fact that, although you may want something badly in your conscious mind, there may be years and years of doubts and limiting beliefs in your subconscious mind. Remember, your subconscious mind runs the show, which is why it must be reprogrammed if it is not in alignment with your conscious desires.
7. Check out *The Automatic Millionaire* by David Bach. When I first started reading books on money, they basically helped me think more positive about it. But I honestly didn't know what practical steps to take at times. This book gave me the first steps to building a better financial future.

7: LOVING LIFE: *The Art of Wonder*

1. I learned this cool exercise from Jen Sincero's book *You Are a Badass.*
2. You can watch this experiment in gratitude here: https: https://www.youtube.com/watch?v=oHv6vTKD6lg.
3. Check out Eckhart Tolle's book *The Power of Now.* It's my favorite book on how to live in the now. Hands down! So go read this book … *now*! (Or after reading my book, of course.)
4. I know these jobs require more than what I'm mentioning. I'm simply highlighting the activities which they are typically known for to make a point.

WANT MORE?

For free access to my videos, blogs and special offers, make sure to sign up for my email list at:
joshuatongol.com

Follow Me:

YouTube
youtube.com/user/joshuat77

Facebook
facebook.com/joshuatongolpage

Twitter
twitter.com/JoshuaTongol

Instagram
instagram.com/joshuatongol

Pinterest
pinterest.com/joshuatongol

Podcast
joshuatongol.podbean.com

P.S.

I'd be honored if you reviewed this book on *Amazon*. Thank you!

SHOUT-OUTS

My awesome family (Ismael, Aurea, Karen, Melorie) - words can't express how grateful I am for all the unconditional love and support you've given me

Chelly and Melorie Cruz - appreciate the feedback and for letting us use your studio. Let's eat?

Lance Salvosa - editor and poetic genius. Thanks for always having my back, homie

Brendon James - designer extraordinaire. Your creativity never ceases to amaze me, brotha

The local Starbucks for being my second "office." You baristas rock! Extra caramel, please

All the b-boys and b-girls on Youtube—as always—who entertained me whenever I needed to take a break (no pun intended) from writing

To those who walked with me when I first started to explore the "miraculous" - you've helped me along the way with my doubts and inspired me to keep moving forward

Remy ... for knowing me like no other

ABOUT THE AUTHOR

Joshua Tongol is a visionary and thought leader who inspires people to dream, take risks and believe the "impossible." He's a popular speaker who has become a fresh voice for modern-day spirituality.

He lives in California with his fun and amazing wife, Remy.

Lightning Source UK Ltd.
Milton Keynes UK
UKOW02f2154041215

264045UK00003B/40/P

9 780991 463954